Crypto Inside

Crypto Inside

Navigating the World of Digital Money

by Meet Patel

**"Dive into the World of Cryptocurrency and Ride the Currents
of Market Trends"**

Disclaimer

This book has been written for information purposes only. Every effort has been made to make this eBook as complete and accurate as possible.

However, there may be mistakes in typography or content. Also, this eBook provides information only up to the publishing date. Therefore, this eBook should be used as a guide - not as the ultimate source.

The purpose of this eBook is to educate. The author and the publisher do not warrant that the information contained in this book is fully complete and shall not be responsible for any errors or omissions.

The author and publisher shall have neither liability nor responsibility to any person or entity with respect to any loss or damage caused or alleged to becaused directly or indirectly by this Book or e-book.

As the author is not a registered financial advisor, it is strongly advisable to conduct your own research before making any investment decisions.

TABLE OF CONTENTS

PREFACE: VOYAGE INTO THE CRYPTO UNIVERSE - UNRAVELING THE REVOLUTIONARY POWER OF DIGITAL FINANCE

Welcome to the captivating world of digital innovation and currency! In this transformative book, "Crypto Inside: Navigating the World of Digital Money," we embark on an exhilarating journey through the revolutionary realm of cryptocurrencies and blockchain technology. Together, we will explore the inner workings of this fascinating landscape, empowering readers of all ages to understand, embrace, and thrive in the era of digital finance.

The dawn of the 21st century ushered in an unprecedented wave of technological advancements, and one remarkable innovation has captured the imagination of millions worldwide – cryptocurrencies. Born out of the curiosity to disrupt traditional financial systems, cryptocurrencies emerged as the pioneers of a decentralized revolution. These digital currencies, free from the clutches of intermediaries, offered a glimpse into a financial future where control and ownership belonged solely to the individual.

As we commence this voyage, let me introduce myself - Meet Patel, your guide through the crypto-verse. Together, we will unlock the mysteries of cryptocurrencies and navigate the ever-changing currents of the digital finance world.

Our journey begins with the foundational concept of blockchain technology, the powerful force underpinning cryptocurrencies. Let's unlock the secrets of how blocks and chains interconnect, record, and fortify transactions, laying the groundwork for the transformative potential of this cutting-edge technology.

Venturing further, we will embark on the adventure of cryptocurrency mining, where computational power plays a crucial role in securing networks and validating transactions. We will traverse both centralized and decentralized exchanges, peering into the mechanics of trading platforms that propel the global crypto market forward.

Beyond the horizon of Bitcoin, the realm of altcoins awaits our discovery. With an immersive exploration of diverse digital currencies, we will comprehend their unique attributes and the distinctive roles they play in the ever-expanding crypto universe.

The rise of decentralized finance (DeFi) captivates our senses, unleashing a new era of financial services that transcends traditional banking paradigms. Together, we will unlock the vast potential of DeFi platforms and applications that redefine the way we interact with money.

Throughout our journey, we will remain vigilant against scams and fraudulent schemes that mar the crypto landscape. Armed with knowledge and insights, we will fortify our defenses and navigate the crypto realm safely.

As we embark on this transformative voyage, we will also explore the contrasting dynamics of proof of work (PoW) and proof of stake (PoS) consensus mechanisms, understanding how these protocols validate and safeguard transactions across diverse blockchains.

Moreover, we will unravel the wonders of smart contracts, self-executing agreements that herald a new era of transparency and trust, transforming industries and igniting a spark of innovation.

This voyage is not just about theory; it's about practical applications too. We will marvel at the possibilities that non-fungible tokens (NFTs) unlock in art, gaming, and beyond, exploring real-world examples that redefine digital ownership.

Throughout our journey, we will be mindful of the evolving regulatory landscape surrounding cryptocurrencies. Examining global approaches to digital asset regulation, we will grasp how regulations impact this dynamic domain.

As we conclude this epic journey, we turn our gaze to the horizon of the future. Emerging trends and innovations will beckon us forward, as we stand poised to embrace the opportunities and challenges that lie ahead.

With "Crypto Inside: Navigating the World of Digital Money," let us embark on an exhilarating quest. Together, we shall unlock the doors to the cryptoverse, empowering ourselves with insights that illuminate the path to a prosperous and decentralized financial future.

So, buckle up and get ready for an adventure like no other. The journey into the crypto universe awaits!

Let the adventure begin!

Meet Patel

ABOUT THE AUTHOR

Meet Patel - a maverick in the world of cutting-edge technology, a fearless explorer of the crypto universe, and a mastermind behind groundbreaking innovations. Armed with a master's in engineering management, Meet is on an unyielding quest to unravel the mysteries of artificial intelligence, while also conquering the thrilling realms of cryptocurrencies.

The siren calls of Bitcoin beckoned Meet in 2016, and like a daring adventurer, he took his first steps into the fascinating world of crypto. However, his initial foray was met with caution, and he sold at a modest profit due to limited knowledge. Yet, Meet's relentless spirit couldn't be subdued. He paused his crypto journey for two years during his bachelor's in mechanical studies, but little did the world know that he was merely honing his skills in the shadows.

With newfound wisdom and fiery determination, Meet's passion reignited, and since 2019, he has been a formidable force in crypto space. Trading, investing, and even crafting ingenious smart contracts for tokens became his second nature. Embracing the art of anonymity, Meet has stealthily collaborated with numerous small token projects, leaving his indelible mark on the evolving crypto landscape.

But that's not all –Meet possesses a rare blend of digital marketing acumen that has propelled his ventures to new heights. A skillful navigator of the online landscape, he has leveraged digital marketing strategies to amplify his presence in the crypto realm. His ability to captivate audiences and drive engagement has made him a force to be reckoned with, ensuring that his innovative projects reach the farthest corners of the cryptoverse.

In a stroke of brilliance, Meet's early instincts led him to invest in SafeMoon, an audacious move that changed the trajectory of his journey forever. But that was just the beginning. His brilliance in trading caught the attention of the crypto community, earning him the coveted title of being among the top 1% traders for Ku Coin Exchange in 2021, and a breathtaking top 2.5% for 2022, culminating in the prestigious "Crypto Warren Buffett" badge.

Beyond his triumphs in the trading arena, Meet's heart beats for innovation. As the intrepid CEO of Cryptvel, a visionary startup based in Australia, he leads a fearless brigade of crypto trailblazers. Their mission: to create and explore uncharted territories in the ever-expanding crypto words.

But Meet is not just a captain of his own ship; he's also a passionate educator. In "Crypto Inside: Navigating the World of Digital Money," he takes readers under his wing, unraveling the cryptoverse with an enthusiasm that's contagious. He believes in democratizing knowledge, ensuring that the cryptoverse's secrets are accessible to all, regardless of their background.

Meet Patel is more than just a name; it's a symbol of audacity, resilience, unwavering determination, and digital marketing prowess. As a tireless explorer of the crypto universe, he seeks to unlock the transformative power of blockchain technology and leave an indelible legacy on the world of cryptocurrencies.

So, again fasten your seatbelts as Meet invites you on an adrenaline-pumping journey into the heart of the crypto realm. Together, we'll ride the waves of innovation, explore uncharted territories, and embrace the untamed spirit of the crypto revolution.

Join Meet Patel - the trailblazer, the visionary, the crypto enthusiast - and embark on an adventure like no other.

SPECIAL THANKS

Gratitude fills my heart as I acknowledge the remarkable souls who have been instrumental in shaping my crypto odyssey.

To my ever-supportive family, Especially my wife **Smiti,** mentors, and friends - your unwavering belief in me has been a guiding light.

To the vibrant crypto community - your passion and knowledge-sharing have kindled my curiosity and spurred me on.

To the dedicated team at **Cryptvel** - your unwavering commitment has turned aspirations into achievements.

To my cherished readers - your enthusiasm fuels my drive to educate and enlighten.

To the trailblazing blockchain pioneers, including Satoshi Nakamoto and Vitalik Buterin - your vision has redefined the realm of possibilities.

To CZ, the founder of Binance - your dedication has transformed the landscape of cryptocurrency exchanges.

And lastly, to the enigmatic forces that bind us all - your mysterious ways have led me on an awe-inspiring journey.

With heartfelt thanks and boundless appreciation,

Meet Patel

CHAPTER 1 INTRODUCTION TO CRYPTOCURRENCIES

Cryptocurrencies are a new form of digital money that uses cryptography to secure transactions and control the creation of new units. Cryptography is the science of encoding and decoding information, using mathematical techniques and algorithms. Cryptocurrencies are also known as crypto assets, digital assets, or simply cryptos.

Cryptocurrencies are different from traditional forms of money, such as cash, bank deposits, or credit cards, in several ways. First, cryptocurrencies are decentralized, meaning that they are not issued or controlled by any central authority, such as a government or a bank. Instead, cryptocurrencies are created and managed by a network of computers, called nodes, that follow a set of rules, called a protocol. Anyone can join the network and participate in the creation and validation of transactions.

Second, cryptocurrencies are transparent, meaning that anyone can see the history and details of every transaction on the network.

Transactions are recorded in a public ledger, called a blockchain, that is shared and synchronized among all nodes. A blockchain is a chain of blocks, where each block contains a batch of transactions and a reference to the previous block. The blockchain ensures that transactions are valid and consistent and prevents double-spending or fraud. Third, cryptocurrencies are scarce, meaning that there is a limited supply of each cryptocurrency. The supply is determined by the protocol and cannot be changed arbitrarily. For example, the protocol of Bitcoin, the first and most popular cryptocurrency, specifies that there will never be more than 21 million bitcoins in existence. The supply of cryptocurrencies creates an incentive for users to mine them, which is the process of using computational power to create new blocks and earn rewards.

Understanding Digital Money and the Blockchain Revolution

Digital money is not a new concept. In fact, most of the money we use today is digital, in the sense that it exists as data in electronic systems, such as bank accounts or payment platforms. However, traditional digital money relies on intermediaries, such as banks or payment processors, to facilitate transactions and ensure trust among parties. These intermediaries charge fees, impose restrictions, and create risks of censorship, fraud, or theft.

The blockchain revolution is the idea that we can create a new kind of digital money that does not depend on intermediaries, but rather on a distributed network of peers that can verify transactions and enforce rules without relying on trust or authority. This is possible thanks to the combination of cryptography and game theory, which enable the creation of secure and incentive-compatible protocols that can coordinate the actions of thousands or millions of nodes.

The blockchain revolution has several implications for the future of money and society. Some of these implications are:

- **Financial inclusion:** Cryptocurrencies can provide access to financial services to billions of people who are unbanked or underbanked, by lowering the barriers to entry and reducing the costs of transactions.

- **Innovation:** Cryptocurrencies can enable new business models, products, and services that were not possible before, such as peer-to-peer lending, decentralized exchanges, smart contracts, or tokenization.

- **Privacy:** Cryptocurrencies can offer users more control over their personal data and financial transactions, by allowing them to transact anonymously or pseudonymously.

- **Sovereignty:** Cryptocurrencies can empower users to have more choice and freedom over their money, by allowing them to store it securely, spend it freely, and hedge against inflation or currency devaluation.

The Promise of Decentralization: Decentralization is one of the core principles and values of cryptocurrencies. Decentralization means that there is no single point of failure or control in the system. Instead, power and responsibility are distributed among multiple actors who act independently but cooperatively.

Decentralization has several benefits for cryptocurrencies and their users. Some of these benefits are:

- **Security:** Decentralization makes the system more resilient to attacks or disruptions, by requiring a majority of nodes to agree on the state of the system.

- **Credibility:** Decentralization makes the system more trustworthy and reliable,

- **Innovation:** Decentralization makes the system more open and adaptable, by allowing anyone to join the network and propose changes or improvements to the protocol.

- **Diversity:** Decentralization makes the system more inclusive and representative, by reflecting the interests and preferences of a wide range of users and stakeholders.

Decentralization is not an absolute or binary concept. Rather, it is a spectrum that can vary depending on different dimensions, such as:

- **Architectural:** How many nodes are involved in the system and how they are connected?

- **Political:** How many entities have influence or authority over the system and how they are governed?

- **Logical:** How many rules or standards are enforced in the system and how they are coordinated?

Different cryptocurrencies have different degrees and forms of decentralization, depending on their design choices and trade-offs. For example, Bitcoin is more decentralized than Ethereum in terms of architecture and politics, but less decentralized than Ethereum in terms of logic. There is no optimal or ideal level of decentralization, as each cryptocurrency has its own goals and challenges.

Decentralization is not a panacea or a guarantee of success. Decentralization also has some drawbacks and limitations, such as:

- **Scalability:** Decentralization can reduce the efficiency and performance of the system, by increasing the complexity and overhead of communication and coordination among nodes.

- **Usability:** Decentralization can increase the difficulty and responsibility of using the system, by requiring users to manage their own keys, wallets, and nodes.

- **Governance:** Decentralization can create conflicts and disputes among the participants of the system, by lacking clear or formal mechanisms for decision-making and dispute resolution.

Decentralization is a dynamic and evolving process that requires constant evaluation and improvement. Decentralization is not an end, but a means to achieve certain objectives and values, such as security, credibility, innovation, and diversity. Decentralization is not only a technical or economic phenomenon but also a social and political one, that reflects the vision and mission of the cryptocurrency community.

IF YOU DON'T BELIEVE IT OR
DON'T GET IT, I DON'T HAVE
THE TIME TO TRY TO
CONVINCE YOU, SORRY.

<u>SATOSHI NAKAMOTO</u>

CHAPTER 2 WHAT IS BLOCKCHAIN?

Blockchain is a technology that allows data to be stored and exchanged on a peer-to-peer (P2P) network. Unlike traditional databases that are centralized and controlled by a single entity, blockchain is decentralized and distributed across multiple nodes (computers) that verify and record transactions. Blockchain can be used to create a secure, transparent, and immutable ledger of data that can be accessed by anyone with permission.

How Blockchain Technology Powers Cryptocurrencies

One of the most popular applications of blockchain technology is cryptocurrencies, such as Bitcoin, Ethereum, and Dogecoin. Cryptocurrencies are digital tokens that can be used as a medium of exchange, store of value, or unit of account on the internet. Cryptocurrencies use blockchain to create a public ledger of all transactions that have ever occurred on the network and to ensure that the tokens are not duplicated or spent more than once.

Cryptocurrencies use cryptographic techniques, such as digital signatures and hash functions, to secure transactions and prevent fraud or tampering. Each transaction is broadcasted to the network and validated by the nodes using a consensus mechanism, such as proof-of-work (PoW) or proof-of-stake (PoS). Once a transaction is confirmed, it is added to a new block of data, which is then linked to the previous block using a hash. This creates a chain of blocks that contains the entire history of transactions on the network.

Cryptocurrencies offer several advantages over traditional currencies, such as lower transaction fees, faster settlement times, greater transparency, and increased financial inclusion. However, they also face some challenges, such as scalability, volatility, regulation, and security.

Exploring the Blocks and Chains

A block is a unit of data that contains information about one or more transactions that have occurred on the blockchain network. A block typically consists of four components:

- A block header, which contains metadata about the block, such as the timestamp, the hash of the previous block, the hash of the current block, and a nonce (a random number used for PoW).

- A transaction counter, which indicates how many

transactions are included in the block.

- A list of transactions, which contains the details of each transaction, such as the sender's address, the receiver's address, the number of tokens transferred, and the digital signature.

- A Merkle root, which is a hash of all the transactions in the block. The Merkle root allows for efficient verification of the transactions without having to download the entire block.

A chain is a sequence of blocks that are linked together using hashes. The first block in the chain is called the genesis block, which is created by the founder or developer of the blockchain network. The genesis block contains no transactions and serves as the origin of the network. The last block in the chain is called the tip or head block, which is updated whenever a new block is added to the chain.

The chain represents the state of the ledger at any given point in time. The chain can be forked into different branches when there are conflicting versions of the ledger among different nodes. Forks can be resolved by applying certain rules or protocols that determine which branch is valid and which branch is discarded.

The chain can also be pruned or compressed to reduce its size and improve its performance. Pruning involves removing old or irrelevant blocks from the chain that are no longer needed for verification purposes. Compression involves using techniques such as sharding or sidechains to split or offload some transactions from the main chain to smaller or parallel chains.

Blockchain Benefits and Challenges: Blockchain technology offers many benefits for various industries and applications, such as:

- **Trustlessness**: Blockchain eliminates the need for intermediaries or trusted third parties, such as banks, brokers, or escrow agents, to verify and facilitate transactions. This reduces the risk of fraud, corruption, or human error, and increases the efficiency and speed of transactions.

- **Transparency**: Blockchain provides a shared and immutable record of all transactions that have ever occurred on the network, which can be accessed by anyone with permission. This enhances the accountability and auditability of the transactions and enables the participants to track the provenance and ownership of the assets.

- **Security**: Blockchain uses cryptographic techniques, such as digital signatures and hash functions, to secure the transactions and prevent unauthorized access or modification of the data. Blockchain also uses consensus mechanisms, such as PoW or PoS, to ensure that the network is synchronized and resistant to attacks or malicious nodes.

- **Innovation**: Blockchain enables the creation of new types of digital assets, such as cryptocurrencies, tokens, NFTs, or smart contracts, that can represent anything of value or logic on the internet. Blockchain also enables the development of new business models, platforms, and applications, such as DeFi, DAOs, or

DApps, that can disrupt existing industries or create new ones.

However, blockchain technology also faces some challenges and limitations, such as:

- **Scalability**: Blockchain has a limited capacity to process transactions per second (TPS), compared to traditional payment systems, such as Visa or PayPal. This is because each transaction must be verified and recorded by all the nodes on the network, which consumes a lot of time and resources. Blockchain also has a trade-off between scalability and security: increasing the block size or reducing the block time can improve the throughput, but also increase the risk of forks or attacks.

- **Volatility**: Blockchain-based assets, such as cryptocurrencies or tokens, are subject to high price fluctuations due to various factors, such as supply and demand, speculation, regulation, or market sentiment. This makes them risky and unpredictable for investors, traders, or users who rely on them for transactions or value storage.

- **Regulation**: Blockchain operates in a legal gray area that varies across different jurisdictions and sectors. There is a lack of clear and consistent rules or standards for blockchain governance, compliance, taxation, and consumer protection. This creates uncertainty and challenges for blockchain developers, users, or regulators who must deal with complex and evolving legal issues.

- **Education**: Blockchain is a complex and novel technology that requires a high level of technical knowledge and skills to understand and use. There is a shortage of blockchain experts, developers, or educators who can provide adequate training or guidance for blockchain adoption. There is also a lack of awareness or trust among the public or potential users who may not fully grasp the benefits or risks of blockchain.

Notes:...

....

....

....

....

....

....

....

....

....

....

....

....

....

....

....

....

....

"CRYPTOCURRENCY IS SUCH A POWERFUL CONCEPT THAT IT CAN ALMOST OVERTURN GOVERNMENTS."

CHARLES LEE

CHAPTER 3 WHAT IS CRYPTOCURRENCY MINING?

Cryptocurrency mining, or crypto mining, is the method of verifying transactions on a digital ledger for a blockchain using machines with extensive computing power. Crypto mining is essential for the security and functionality of many cryptocurrencies, such as Bitcoin, Ethereum, and Dogecoin.

The Process of Mining and Its Role in Blockchain Security

Crypto mining is the process where specialized computers, also known as nodes or mining rigs, validate blockchain transactions for a specific crypto coin and, in turn, receive a mining reward for their computational effort.

Crypto mining is how miners compete to prove their computational work in exchange for a block reward. After a series of transactions for a specific cryptocurrency, a block with associated cryptographic hash functions containing transaction data becomes visible to the blockchain's P2P network.

The miners then use their mining rigs to solve a complex mathematical puzzle that involves the hash of the previous block, and a random number called a nonce. The first miner who finds the correct solution broadcasts it to the network and gets the block reward, which consists of newly created coins and transaction fees.

The other miners then verify the solution and add the new block to their copy of the ledger. This creates a chain of blocks that contains the entire history of transactions on the network. The longer the chain, the more secure and immutable it becomes.

Crypto mining plays a vital role in blockchain security by:

- **Preventing double-spending**: Crypto mining ensures that each coin can only be spent once by recording every transaction on the ledger and making it irreversible.

- **Maintaining consensus**: Crypto mining ensures that all nodes on the network agree on the same version of the ledger by following certain rules or protocols that determine which block is valid and which block is discarded.

- **Deterring attacks**: Crypto mining makes it difficult and costly for attackers to alter or manipulate the ledger by requiring them to have more computing power than many honest miners.

Real-World Mining Examples and Their Impact

Crypto mining can be done by anyone who has access to a suitable mining rig and an internet connection. However, crypto mining is not easy or cheap: it requires a lot of electricity, cooling, maintenance, and technical knowledge.

Some examples of real-world crypto mining are:

- **Individual mining**: Some people mine cryptocurrencies using their personal computers or laptops, or by buying dedicated hardware devices such as ASICs (application-specific integrated circuits) or GPUs (graphics processing units). Individual mining can be profitable if the miner has low electricity costs, high-performance equipment, and favorable market conditions.

- **Pool mining**: Some people join forces with other miners and form pools, where they share their computing power and split the rewards according to their contribution. Pool mining can increase the chances of finding a block and reduce the variance of earnings. However, pool mining also involves paying fees to the pool operator and trusting them to distribute the rewards fairly.

- **Cloud mining**: Some people rent computing power from third-party providers who own and operate large-scale mining farms. Cloud mining can eliminate the hassle and cost of buying and maintaining mining equipment. However, cloud mining also involves paying fees to the provider and trusting them to deliver the promised service.

Crypto mining has various impacts on society and the environment, such as:

- **Economic impact**: Crypto mining creates new income opportunities for individuals and businesses who participate in or provide services for the crypto industry. Crypto mining also stimulates innovation and competition in the fields of hardware, software, and energy efficiency.

- **Social impact**: Crypto mining enables financial inclusion and empowerment for people who lack access to traditional banking or payment systems. Crypto mining also fosters community building and collaboration among crypto enthusiasts who share common values and goals.

- **Environmental impact**: Crypto mining consumes a lot of electricity, which may contribute to greenhouse gas emissions and climate change if it comes from fossil fuels. Crypto mining also generates a lot of heat and noise, which may affect the quality of life of nearby residents.

Statistics on Bitcoin Mining and Energy Consumption in 2023

Highlights of Bitcoin Mining Statistics

- The annual global electricity consumption of Bitcoin mining was roughly 95.58 terawatt-hours in May 2023.

- Bitcoin is thought to account for 60-77% of global crypto-asset electricity use.

- Bitcoin mining has a market capitalization of $8.11 billion.

- Bitcoin miners make $27.70 million in daily revenue.

- The United States has the world's largest Bitcoin mining sector, accounting for more than 38% of the worldwide Bitcoin network's hash rate.

Bitcoin Mining Energy Consumption Statistics

Bitcoin mining energy use has sparked much interest and investigation. As Bitcoin's popularity and value have grown, so has the amount of energy required to generate new currencies and maintain the network.

According to the New York Times, Bitcoin mining consumes about 0.5% of global energy production.

The electricity consumed in the state of Washington is comparable to more than a third of the electricity used for household cooling in the United States each year.

Furthermore, the electricity utilized by Bitcoin mining is more than seven times greater than the total energy consumption of Google's global operations.

In the early days of Bitcoin, when it had a little following, a single desktop computer could easily mine the cryptocurrency in seconds.

According to the same research, it takes around "9 years of typical household electricity" to mine a single bitcoin.

Bitcoin mining was predicted to consume approximately 95.58 terawatt-hours of electricity in May 2023.

Its annual electricity usage peaked at 204.5 terawatt-hours in 2022, exceeding Finland's power consumption.

China Bans Bitcoin Mining

When it comes to ranking countries in Bitcoin mining, China, the United States, and Kazakhstan are the most frequently mentioned. China has shut it down, making Bitcoin mining illegal in many countries.

Bitcoin trading is a type of cryptocurrency transaction in which Bitcoin serves as a digital marker on a digital ledger known as a blockchain. Making money through currency exchange is a practice employed by investors all over the world, and it is fully legal when stated and taxed. Bitcoin mining is a method of earning money by solving a mathematical equation. By using this mathematical technique, one miner can earn a block of bitcoin in ten minutes and $250,000 in just one hour. That much time. China shut it down, which shook the Bitcoin mining industry, but China regarded it as a threat to the entire economy.

Bitcoin mining is not regulated in the United States.

When it comes to bitcoin mining by country, America ranks first, making it legal. It's no different in our country than going to the bank with money from one country and cashing it in for additional money from another. Miners with a math gene will do well in New York and Texas, which are two of the most popular places in America to mine Bitcoin.

The infrastructure required for miners to conduct their task is relatively inexpensive, and it consists of a gadget, a Wi-Fi connection, and electricity. It's not difficult to learn, and America provides the necessary tools and support for aspiring miners.

Kazakhstan Mines Bitcoin in Exchange for Coal

Kazakhstan is a bitcoin miner fueled by coal because coal is inexpensive, and its power efficiency drives the country's bitcoin mining activity. It also has a desert where 50,000 computers are set up in Ekibastuz to help the miners get it down.

Bitcoin miners in this location perform 12-hour shifts for two weeks straight until the bitcoin is mined. This is unlikely to be criminalized anytime soon, given Kazakhstan's position as a world leader in this business.

How Does Bitcoin Work?

Bitcoin is measured in hash rate units, which refer to how quickly a computation may perform on a machine each second. The network is used to create and process a transaction. The greater the hash rate, the greater the profit. The top Bitcoin mining countries and hash rates are as follows:

- 35.4% in the United States
- 18.1% Kazakhstan

- Russia has an 11.23% share.

- Canada has a rate of 9.55%.

- Ireland: 4.68 percent

- Malaysia (4.58%).

- Germany has 4.48%.

- Iran: 3.1%

Data on Bitcoin Mining Revenue

As of June 26, 2023, the daily revenue generated by Bitcoin miners stands at $27.70 million, up from $18.20 million in the previous 12 months.

This is a considerable increase of 52.20% over the previous year's similar period.

Bitcoin miners had their biggest daily earnings since 2018 in April 2021, totaling $80.12 million.

Bitcoin Miners Earnings

According to Glassnode, Bitcoin miners observed an unusually large exchange interaction of $128 million in a single transaction on June 27, 2023.

This amount is a whopping 315% of their daily revenue.

Bitcoin Mining Revenue Sources

- Bitcoin Block Rewards and transaction fees are the two main sources of income for miners. Miners who successfully mine a block in the blockchain system receive Bitcoin incentives. To claim the reward, the miner places it at the beginning of the block.

•	Every four years, the reward for successfully mining a block in the Bitcoin network is halved, effectively cutting it in half.

•	When Bitcoin first appeared, the block reward for mining was set at 50 bitcoins.

•	The mining payout for each block of transactions is 6.25 Bitcoins as of June 2023, and it occurs around every 10 minutes. The next halving is scheduled for 2024. The block reward will be reduced to 3.125 BTC as a result.

CHAPTER 4 WHAT ARE CENTRALIZED AND DECENTRALIZED EXCHANGES?

Cryptocurrencies are digital assets that can be used to buy, sell, or trade goods and services on the internet. However, to do so, you need a platform that allows you to exchange one cryptocurrency for another, or for fiat currency (such as US dollars or euros). These platforms are called cryptocurrency exchanges.

Cryptocurrency exchanges can be classified into two main types: centralized and decentralized. In this chapter, we will explore the differences between these two types of exchanges, their advantages and disadvantages, and some real-world examples of each.

Understanding How Exchanges Facilitate Crypto Trading

A cryptocurrency exchange is a platform that connects buyers and sellers of cryptocurrencies. It provides the necessary infrastructure, such as order books, matching engines, wallets, and payment systems, to enable users to conduct transactions.

A cryptocurrency exchange can offer different services, such as:

- **Spot trading**: This is the most common type of service, where users can buy or sell cryptocurrencies at the current market price.

- **Margin trading**: This is a type of service where users can borrow funds from the exchange or other users to trade with leverage, meaning they can amplify their profits or losses.

- **Futures trading**: This is a type of service where users can enter contracts that oblige them to buy or sell a certain amount of cryptocurrency at a predetermined price and date in the future.

- **Lending and borrowing**: This is a type of service where users can lend or borrow cryptocurrencies from the exchange or other users and earn interest or pay fees.

- **Staking and farming**: This is a type of service where users can lock up their cryptocurrencies in the exchange or in smart contracts and earn rewards for contributing to network security or liquidity.

A cryptocurrency exchange can also offer different features, such as:

- **Trading tools**: These are tools that help users analyze market trends, execute orders, manage risks, and optimize their strategies.

- **Customer support**: This is a service that helps users with any issues or inquiries they may have regarding the exchange or their transactions.

- **Security measures**: These are the measures that protect the exchange and its users from hackers, fraudsters, or malicious actors.

- **Regulatory compliance**: This is the service that ensures the exchange follows the rules and regulations of the jurisdictions where it operates or serves its customers.

Differences Between Centralized and Decentralized Platforms

The main difference between centralized and decentralized exchanges is the degree of involvement of a third party in facilitating the transactions.

A centralized exchange relies on intermediaries to oversee the transactions of users on its system. However, a decentralized exchange relies on technology, such as smart contracts or peer-to-peer networks, to enable direct transactions between users without intermediaries.

The following table summarizes some of the key differences between centralized and decentralized exchanges:

Centralized Exchange	Decentralized Exchange
Control	The exchange has control over the user's funds, data, and transactions.
Security	The exchange is responsible for securing the user's funds and data from hackers or theft. However, if the exchange gets hacked or compromised, the user could lose their funds or data.
Fees	The exchange charges fees for its services, such as trading fees, withdrawal fees, deposit fees, etc.
Variety	The exchange offers a variety of cryptocurrencies and trading pairs that it supports and lists. However, it may also delist some cryptocurrencies due to regulatory or other reasons.
Risks	The user faces risks such as hacking, fraud, censorship, downtime, or insolvency of the exchange.

Centralized Exchange	Decentralized Exchange
Regulation	The exchange is subject to regulation by financial authorities and must comply with KYC (know your customer) and AML (anti-money laundering) rules. This may affect the privacy and accessibility of the user.
Liquidity	The exchange provides high liquidity and allows users to conduct trades up to tens or hundreds of millions of dollars for the most liquid cryptocurrencies.

Centralized Exchange Examples and Their Impact

Some examples of centralized exchanges are:

- **Binance:** This is the largest and most popular centralized exchange in terms of trading volume and users. It offers a wide range of services, such as spot trading, margin trading, futures trading, lending, and borrowing, staking and farming, and more. It also supports over 300 cryptocurrencies and thousands of trading pairs. Binance is known for its low fees, high liquidity, and user-friendly interface.

- **Coinbase:** This is the largest and most reputable centralized exchange in the US. It offers a simple and secure platform for buying and selling cryptocurrencies with fiat currency. It also provides other services, such as Coinbase Pro, Coinbase Wallet, Coinbase Earn, Coinbase Commerce, and more. It supports over 50 cryptocurrencies and hundreds of trading pairs. Coinbase is known for its regulatory compliance, customer support, and educational resources.

- **Kraken:** This is one of the oldest and most respected centralized exchanges in the world. It offers a robust and reliable platform for trading cryptocurrencies with fiat currency or other cryptocurrencies. It also provides other services, such as margin trading, futures trading, staking, lending, and borrowing, and more. It supports over 60 cryptocurrencies and hundreds of trading pairs. Kraken is known for its security measures, customer service, and transparency.

Centralized exchanges have various impacts on the crypto industry and society, such as:

- **Economic impact:** Centralized exchanges create new income opportunities for their owners, employees, partners, and customers. They also stimulate innovation and competition in the fields of technology, finance, and business.

- **Social impact:** Centralized exchanges enable financial inclusion and empowerment for people who can access their services. They also foster community building and collaboration among crypto enthusiasts who share common values and goals.

- **Environmental impact:** Centralized exchanges consume a lot of electricity to power their servers and operations. This may contribute to greenhouse gas emissions and climate change if they use non-renewable energy sources. However, some centralized exchanges are taking steps to reduce their environmental footprint by using renewable energy sources or offsetting their emissions.

Decentralized Exchange Examples and Their Impact

Some examples of decentralized exchanges are:

- **Uniswap:** This is the largest and most popular decentralized exchange on Ethereum. It uses an automated market maker (AMM) model to facilitate liquidity provision and price discovery for any ERC-20 token pair. It also allows users to create their own pools or swap tokens without intermediaries or fees. Uniswap is known for its simplicity, efficiency, and innovation.

- **Pancake Swap:** This is the largest and most popular decentralized exchange on Binance Smart Chain. It uses a similar AMM model to Uniswap but with lower fees and faster transactions. It also offers other features, such as a lottery, prediction market, NFT marketplace, farms, pools, and more. PancakeSwap is known for its gamification, community, and rewards.

- **SushiSwap:** This is a fork of Uniswap that aims to improve its governance and incentives. It uses the same AMM model as Uniswap but with a token called SUSHI that gives holders voting rights and a share of the fees generated by the platform. It also offers other features, such as lending and borrowing, margin trading, limit orders, NFTs, farms, pools, and more. SushiSwap is known for its innovation, diversity, and collaboration.

Decentralized exchanges have various impacts on the crypto industry and society, such as:

- **Economic impact:** Decentralized exchanges create new income opportunities for their developers, users, liquidity providers, token holders, and partners. They also stimulate innovation and competition in the fields of technology, finance, and business.

- **Social impact:** Decentralized exchanges enable financial inclusion and empowerment for people who can access their services without censorship or intermediation. They also foster community building and collaboration among crypto enthusiasts who share common values and goals.

- **Environmental impact:** Decentralized exchanges consume a lot of electricity to run their smart contracts and transactions on the blockchain. This may contribute to greenhouse gas emissions and climate change if they use non-renewable energy sources. However, some decentralized exchanges are taking steps to reduce their environmental footprint by using layer 2 solutions or alternative blockchains that are more energy efficient.

History of Bitcoin

Unveiling Bitcoin: A Comprehensive Exploration

Imagine a digital currency that doesn't rely on banks or governments, a currency you can send anywhere in the world with just a few clicks. That's Bitcoin, and it's changing the way we think about money. Let's dive into this exciting world and understand what Bitcoin all is about.

1. The Birth of Bitcoin

Bitcoin emerged in 2009 when an unknown person or group using the pseudonym Satoshi Nakamoto released a whitepaper titled "Bitcoin: A Peer-to-Peer Electronic Cash System." This whitepaper introduced the concept of a decentralized digital currency that operates on a secure and transparent network called the blockchain.

2. Digital Gold

Think of Bitcoin as digital gold. Just as gold has value because it's rare and desirable, Bitcoin's value comes from its scarcity and the belief that it can be a store of value. There will only ever be 21 million Bitcoins, making it deflationary in nature.

3. How Bitcoin Works

At its core, Bitcoin is a peer-to-peer network where transactions are recorded on a public ledger called the blockchain. When you send Bitcoin to someone, the transaction is verified by network participants called miners. Once verified, the transaction is added to a block, which is linked to the previous block, forming a chain of blocks – the blockchain.

4. Mining and Rewards

Mining is the process by which new Bitcoins are created and transactions are confirmed. Miners use powerful computers to solve complex mathematical puzzles. The first miner to solve the puzzle gets to add the next block to the blockchain and is rewarded with newly minted Bitcoins and transaction fees.

5. Wallets and Addresses

To use Bitcoin, you need a digital wallet. This wallet contains a pair of cryptographic keys: a public key, which is like your address, and a private key, which is your secret password. Your public key is what you share to receive Bitcoin, and your private key is what you use to access and manage your funds securely.

6. Peer-to-Peer Transactions

Sending Bitcoin is as easy as sending an email. You enter the recipient's address and the amount you want to send, and with a few clicks, the transaction is broadcast to the network. Within minutes, the recipient can see the Bitcoin in their wallet.

7. Beyond Money: Smart Contracts

Bitcoin isn't just about digital money; it's also a platform for innovation. Smart contracts are self-executing contracts with the terms of the agreement directly written into code. They enable various applications, from decentralized finance to creating digital assets representing ownership of real-world items.

8. The Bitcoin Community

Bitcoin has a passionate global community of developers, miners, traders, and enthusiasts. This community drives the development of Bitcoin, debates its future, and collaborates on improvements to the network.

9. Challenges and Future

Bitcoin isn't without challenges. Its price can be extremely volatile, and regulatory uncertainties exist in some parts of the world. However, Bitcoin's potential to disrupt traditional financial systems and empower individuals with financial sovereignty is undeniable.

The Evolution of Bitcoin: From Concept to Cryptocurrency

Now that we have a basic understanding of what Bitcoin is, let's explore its journey from a revolutionary concept to a full-fledged cryptocurrency that has transformed the way we perceive money and technology.

1. Early Days and Adoption

When Bitcoin was first introduced by Satoshi Nakamoto in 2009, it was met with curiosity but limited adoption. Early enthusiasts and tech-savvy individuals started mining and trading Bitcoin, but its potential was not fully understood by the general public.

2. Media Attention and Growth

Around 2013, Bitcoin started gaining more media attention, leading to a surge in interest. People realized that this digital currency had the potential to disrupt traditional financial systems and empower individuals with greater control over their money.

3. Price Volatility and Speculation

Bitcoin's price journey has been marked by extreme volatility. In the early years, its value was minimal, but in 2017, its price experienced a historic bull run, reaching nearly $20,000 per Bitcoin. This led to both excitement and concerns about a potential bubble.

4. Technological Improvements

As more people became interested in Bitcoin, developers started working on improvements to address its scalability and usability issues. Segregated Witness (SegWit) and the Lightning Network are examples of technological advancements aimed at enhancing transaction speed and reducing fees.

5. Mainstream Acceptance

Over the years, Bitcoin has achieved a level of mainstream acceptance. Some businesses and online retailers started accepting Bitcoin as a form of payment. Additionally, financial institutions and governments began to acknowledge its significance and explore ways to regulate it.

6. Global Impact

Bitcoin has made a significant impact worldwide. In countries with unstable economies or limited access to traditional banking, Bitcoin offers an alternative way for people to store value and engage in financial transactions.

7. Regulatory Challenges

The decentralized and pseudonymous nature of Bitcoin has led to regulatory challenges. Different countries have taken varied approaches to regulate or restrict Bitcoin usage. Some governments embraced it, while others-imposed bans or strict regulations.

8. Innovations and Beyond

Bitcoin's success has paved the way for the development of thousands of other cryptocurrencies and blockchain projects. It also introduced the concept of blockchain technology, which has applications beyond just digital currency – from supply chain management to healthcare.

9. Community and Collaboration

Bitcoin has a passionate and diverse community that includes developers, miners, traders, academics, and enthusiasts. This community collaborates to improve the Bitcoin network, address challenges, and explore new possibilities.

10. Looking Ahead

The future of Bitcoin holds both excitement and uncertainty. Technological advancements, regulatory developments, and market trends will continue to shape its trajectory. As it evolves, Bitcoin will likely play a crucial role in shaping the future of finance and technology.

Bitcoin Deconstructed: Unraveling Its Core Mechanisms

Now that we've explored the journey and basics of Bitcoin, let's delve deeper into the inner workings of this revolutionary digital currency. Understanding its core mechanisms will give us a clearer picture of how Bitcoin functions and why it's so unique.

1. Blockchain: The Digital Ledger

At the heart of Bitcoin lies the blockchain, a digital ledger that records all transactions in a secure and transparent manner. Imagine it as a chain of blocks, with each block containing a list of transactions. Once a block is added, it's linked to the previous block, forming an unalterable chain.

2. Mining: Securing the Network

Bitcoin transactions are verified and added to the blockchain through a process called mining. Miners use powerful computers to solve complex mathematical puzzles. When a puzzle is solved, the miner adds a new block of transactions to the blockchain and is rewarded with new Bitcoins and transaction fees.

3. Consensus Mechanism: Proof of Work

Bitcoin's consensus mechanism, called Proof of Work (PoW), ensures that all network participants agree on the validity of transactions. Miners compete to solve mathematical puzzles, and the first one to solve it gets to add the block. This process makes it computationally intensive and requires a lot of energy.

4. Decentralization: No Central Authority

Unlike traditional currencies controlled by central banks, Bitcoin operates on a decentralized network. No single entity has control over the entire network, making it resistant to censorship and manipulation.

5. Limited Supply: Deflationary Nature

Bitcoin's scarcity is one of its defining features. With a maximum supply of 21 million coins, it's designed to be deflationary over time, in contrast to traditional fiat currencies that can be printed indefinitely.

6. Digital Signatures: Ensuring Security

Every Bitcoin transaction is secured using digital signatures. These signatures ensure that only the rightful owner of a Bitcoin wallet can access and transfer the funds.

7. Private and Public Keys: Your Digital Identity

To use Bitcoin, you need a pair of cryptographic keys – a public key and a private key. The public key is like your address, and you share it to receive funds. The private key is your secret password and must be kept secure, as it gives you control over your funds.

8. Wallets: Safeguarding Your Bitcoins

Bitcoin wallets come in various forms: software, hardware, mobile, and paper wallets. They enable you to store and manage your Bitcoins securely, with different levels of convenience and security.

9. Transactions and Confirmations

When you send Bitcoin to someone, the transaction is broadcast to the network. Miners then include it in a block, and once the block is added to the blockchain, the transaction is confirmed. The more confirmations a transaction has, the more secure it becomes.

10. Challenges and Improvements

While Bitcoin has introduced revolutionary concepts, it's not without challenges. Scalability, energy consumption, and user experience are areas that developers are continually working on to improve.

Bitcoin's Impact: Transforming Finance and Beyond

As we continue our exploration of Bitcoin, let's delve into the profound impact it has had on various aspects of our lives. From finance to technology, Bitcoin's influence extends far beyond being just a digital currency.

1. Financial Inclusion and Accessibility

One of Bitcoin's most significant contributions is improving financial inclusion. In regions with limited access to traditional banking, Bitcoin offers a way for individuals to store value and engage in transactions without relying on physical infrastructure.

2. Remittances and Cross-Border Transactions

Bitcoin has revolutionized the way remittances are sent across borders. Traditional methods involve high fees and lengthy processes. With Bitcoin, cross-border transactions can be completed faster and at a lower cost, benefiting immigrants and their families.

3. Banking the Unbanked

A large portion of the world's population lacks access to

banking services. Bitcoin provides an opportunity for individuals to become their own banks, holding and managing their funds directly through digital wallets.

4. Empowering Individuals with Financial Sovereignty

Bitcoin gives users greater control over their finances. With traditional banking, your funds are subject to regulations and can be frozen or seized. Bitcoin allows you to have full ownership and control of your wealth.

5. Hedge Against Inflation

In countries experiencing hyperinflation or economic instability, Bitcoin offers a hedge against the devaluation of traditional currencies. People can convert their savings into Bitcoin to preserve their wealth.

6. Decentralized Finance (DeFi)

The concept of DeFi leverages blockchain technology and cryptocurrencies to recreate traditional financial services without intermediaries. Smart contracts on the Ethereum blockchain, for example, enable lending, borrowing, and trading without banks.

7. Innovation and Entrepreneurship

Bitcoin's open nature has sparked innovation. Startups and entrepreneurs are developing applications ranging from secure voting systems to digital identity verification, all built on the principles of blockchain technology.

8. Public Awareness and Education

Bitcoin's rise has prompted discussions about the nature of money, the potential of blockchain, and the future of finance. It's driving public awareness about technology, economics, and the importance of financial literacy.

9. Criticisms and Concerns

While Bitcoin's impact is largely positive, it also faces criticisms. Some concerns include its environmental footprint due to energy-intensive mining and its potential misuse in illegal activities.

10. The Path Forward

As Bitcoin continues to evolve, it's crucial for society to engage in discussions about its potential benefits and challenges. Innovations like the Lightning Network aim to improve scalability and speed, making Bitcoin more suitable for everyday transactions.

Bitcoin's Future: Innovations, Challenges, and Beyond

In our final exploration of Bitcoin, we'll peer into the future to understand the potential innovations, challenges, and the role

Bitcoin may play in shaping the world in the years to come.

1. Technological Innovations

Bitcoin's journey is far from over. Developers are continuously working on technological improvements to address its scalability, energy consumption, and transaction speed. Innovations like the Lightning Network aim to make micro-transactions faster and cheaper.

2. Institutional Adoption

As Bitcoin gains legitimacy and recognition, more institutional investors are entering the space. Investment firms, hedge funds, and even some publicly traded companies are allocating a portion of their portfolios to Bitcoin, which further validates its potential as a store of value.

3. Central Bank Digital Currencies (CBDCs)

Central banks in several countries are exploring the idea of creating their own digital currencies. These Central Bank Digital Currencies (CBDCs) could work alongside Bitcoin and other cryptocurrencies, potentially reshaping the global financial landscape.

4. Environmental Concerns and Solutions

Bitcoin's energy consumption, particularly its Proof of Work consensus mechanism, has raised environmental concerns.

However, the community is actively working on solutions to make the network more energy-efficient and sustainable.

5. Financial Inclusion and Developing Economies

Bitcoin's impact on financial inclusion could be profound, especially in developing economies. By providing access to a global financial system, Bitcoin has the potential to empower individuals who are currently excluded from traditional banking.

6. Regulatory Landscape

As Bitcoin gains traction, governments and regulatory bodies are trying to establish frameworks to address its use. Striking a balance between regulation and innovation is a challenge that will shape the future of Bitcoin's integration into mainstream finance.

7. Privacy and Security Enhancements

Enhancing privacy features while maintaining compliance with regulations is a delicate balance. Privacy-focused cryptocurrencies are emerging, aiming to provide users with more control over their personal information.

8. Education and Awareness

As Bitcoin becomes a more integral part of our financial landscape, education and awareness will play a crucial role. Initiatives to promote financial literacy and responsible use of Bitcoin will be essential.

9. International Transactions and Remittances

Bitcoin's potential to revolutionize cross-border transactions and remittances remains a compelling use case. As more individuals recognize the benefits of borderless and low-cost transactions, Bitcoin's role in international finance could grow.

10. Collaboration and Community

Bitcoin's future is intertwined with the collaborative efforts of its global community. As stakeholders work together to address challenges and drive innovation, Bitcoin's potential impact continues to expand.

CHAPTER 5 WHAT IS ALTCOIN?

Exploring Different Types of Altcoins

While Bitcoin might be the most well-known cryptocurrency, it's just the tip of the iceberg in the world of digital currencies. Altcoins, short for "alternative coins," encompass a diverse range of cryptocurrencies that have emerged after Bitcoin. In this section, we'll take a closer look at different types of altcoins and how they bring their unique features to the table.

The Altcoin Landscape

Altcoins are essentially any cryptocurrencies other than Bitcoin. They were developed with the goal of addressing certain limitations of Bitcoin or introducing new functionalities. Some altcoins aim to improve upon the speed of transactions, enhance privacy, enable smart contracts, or serve specific industries. Here are a few categories of altcoins:

- **Litecoin (LTC):** Often referred to as "silver to Bitcoin's gold," Litecoin was one of the earliest altcoins. It offers faster transaction confirmation times and a different hashing algorithm.

- **Ethereum (ETH):** Ethereum is not just a cryptocurrency; it's also a platform for creating and running decentralized applications (DApps) and smart contracts. This innovation allowed developers to build complex applications on its blockchain.

- **Ripple (XRP):** Ripple focuses on enabling fast and cost-effective cross-border payments for financial institutions. It aims to bridge the gap between traditional finance and the blockchain world.

- **Monero (XMR):** Monero places a strong emphasis on privacy and anonymity. Transactions on the Monero blockchain are designed to be untraceable and unlinkable.

- **Cardano (ADA):** Cardano aims to create a more balanced and sustainable blockchain ecosystem through a scientific and research-driven approach.

- **Polkadot (DOT):** Polkadot introduces interoperability between different blockchains, allowing them to share information and assets more easily.

- **Chainlink (LINK):** Chainlink focuses on enabling smart contracts to interact with real-world data, opening new possibilities for decentralized applications.

Understanding Tokenomics

Altcoins often introduce their own native tokens, which serve various purposes within their respective ecosystems. These tokens can have different functions, such as providing access to platform features, representing ownership in a project, or serving as a medium of exchange within a specific application.

For example, Ethereum's native token, Ether (ETH), is used to fuel transactions and execute smart contracts on the Ethereum network. In contrast, Ripple's XRP is used to facilitate cross-border transactions on its network.

Navigating the Altcoin Market

Investing in altcoins offers opportunities for diversification and exposure to various blockchain projects. However, the altcoin market is highly volatile and can be more unpredictable than traditional investment markets. Here are a few considerations:

- **Research:** Thoroughly research the altcoin you're interested in. Understand its purpose, technology, team, and potential use cases.

- **Volatility:** Be prepared for significant price fluctuations. Altcoin prices can soar and crash within a short period.

- **Use Cases:** Evaluate whether the altcoin has a clear use case and addresses a specific problem or need.

- **Team and Development:** Assess the team's qualifications and the progress of the project's development. A strong team can significantly impact the success of an altcoin.

- **Market Adoption:** Consider whether the altcoin has gained traction and adoption within its target industry or community.

Evaluating the Potential of Altcoin Investments

As the cryptocurrency market continues to evolve, many investors are drawn to altcoins as potential investment opportunities. However, before diving into the world of altcoin investments, it's crucial to understand the factors that can influence their potential and the considerations you should keep in mind.

Factors Influencing Altcoin Potential

- **Use Case and Utility:** One of the primary factors that determine the potential of an altcoin is its use case. Does the altcoin address a real-world problem or offer a unique solution? Altcoins with clear and practical use cases tend to have higher potential for adoption and value.

- **Technology and Innovation:** The underlying technology of an altcoin plays a significant role. Innovative features, such as smart contract capabilities or enhanced privacy, can set an altcoin apart and attract both developers and users.

- **Market Demand:** The demand for an altcoin within a specific industry or community can influence its value. If the altcoin solves a problem or fulfills a need in a growing market, it's more likely to gain traction.

- **Team and Development:** The team behind an altcoin is crucial. Experienced and reputable developers, advisors, and leaders contribute to the altcoin's credibility and potential for success.

- **Community and Adoption:** A strong and engaged community can foster adoption and development. Communities that actively support and promote the altcoin can positively impact its growth.

Considerations for Altcoin Investments

- **Diversification:** While altcoin investments can be rewarding, they also come with higher risks. Diversifying your investment portfolio across different altcoins reduces the impact of potential losses from a single investment.

- **Research:** Thoroughly research the altcoins you're considering. Understand their whitepapers, technology, development progress, and any partnerships they have formed.

- **Long-Term Perspective:** Altcoin investments are often more successful when approached with a long-term perspective. Short-term price fluctuations are common, but a strong altcoin with a solid foundation can appreciate over time.

- **Risk Management:** Due to the volatility of the cryptocurrency market, it's important to invest only what you can afford to lose. Avoid investing large portions of your savings or assets.

- **Stay Updated:** The cryptocurrency market is dynamic, with new developments, partnerships, and regulatory changes affecting altcoin values. Stay informed about market trends and news.

Navigating the Risks

It's important to note that altcoin investments come with risks that investors need to be aware of:

- **Volatility:** Altcoins are known for their price volatility. Prices can experience rapid and significant fluctuations, which can lead to both gains and losses.

- **Regulatory Uncertainty:** The regulatory environment for cryptocurrencies varies by country and can change rapidly. Regulatory developments can impact the value and legality of altcoins.

- **Market Manipulation:** The relatively young and unregulated nature of the cryptocurrency market can make it susceptible to market manipulation.

- **Liquidity:** Some altcoins may have lower liquidity, meaning it can be challenging to buy or sell them quickly without significantly affecting their price.

Altcoin Adoption and the Future of Digital Currencies

As the cryptocurrency landscape continues to evolve, the adoption and integration of altcoins into various industries and use cases are shaping the future of digital currencies. In this section, we'll explore how altcoin adoption is changing the way we perceive and interact with financial systems and technology.

Altcoin Adoption Across Industries

Altcoins are finding applications across diverse industries, beyond just the financial sector:

- **Supply Chain Management:** Altcoins are used to track and verify the authenticity of goods as they move through the supply chain, ensuring transparency and preventing counterfeiting.

- **Healthcare:** Altcoins are facilitating secure and private sharing of medical records and data between patients, doctors, and healthcare providers.

- **Gaming:** Altcoins enable in-game purchases, ownership of virtual assets, and the creation of decentralized gaming platforms.

- **Real Estate:** Altcoins are used to streamline property transactions, reducing the need for intermediaries, and enhancing security.

Altcoin Innovations

Altcoins are often developed with specific innovations that set them apart from traditional cryptocurrencies:

- **Smart Contracts:** Altcoins like Ethereum introduced the concept of smart contracts, which are self-executing agreements with terms directly written into code. These contracts automate and enforce transactions without the need for intermediaries.

- **Privacy Features:** Altcoins like Monero and Zcash focus on enhancing privacy and anonymity in transactions, allowing users to keep their financial activities confidential.

- **Interoperability:** Altcoins like Polkadot aim to facilitate communication and data sharing between different blockchains, enabling a more interconnected and efficient ecosystem.

Challenges to Altcoin Adoption

While altcoins offer a promising future, several challenges need to be addressed for widespread adoption:

Regulation: Altcoins face regulatory challenges as governments and financial institutions grapple with their legal status and potential impact on financial systems.

Scalability: Some altcoins struggle with scalability as they aim to accommodate a growing number of users and transactions on their networks.

Usability: To achieve mass adoption, altcoins need to be user-friendly and accessible to individuals who may not be familiar with blockchain technology.

The Role of Altcoins in Finance

Altcoins are challenging traditional financial systems by offering alternatives that are more accessible, transparent, and inclusive. They enable individuals to have more control over their financial transactions and assets, reducing the need for intermediaries like banks.

The Future of Digital Currencies

The future of digital currencies is likely to be a diverse ecosystem where various altcoins coexist with traditional fiat currencies. Altcoins have the potential to reshape industries, improve financial inclusion, and enhance the efficiency of global transactions.

Conclusion

Altcoins are more than just alternatives to Bitcoin; they represent the evolution of blockchain technology and the potential to transform various aspects of our lives. As altcoins gain adoption and showcase innovative features, they contribute to the growth of the cryptocurrency landscape. While challenges remain, the future of digital currencies looks promising, with altcoins playing a crucial role in shaping a more decentralized and interconnected world.

Ethereum Unveiled

A Comprehensive Exploration

Imagine a platform that goes beyond just being a digital currency. A platform where you can build decentralized applications, create digital assets, and even execute self-executing contracts. This is Ethereum, a blockchain technology that has taken the world of cryptocurrencies to a whole new level. Let's dive into the fascinating world of Ethereum and understand what it's all about.

1. The Birth of Ethereum

Ethereum was proposed by a young programmer named Vitalik Buterin in late 2013. It was officially launched in 2015 after a successful crowdfunding campaign. Ethereum aimed to expand the capabilities of blockchain beyond simply being a ledger for cryptocurrencies like Bitcoin.

2. Beyond Digital Currency

While Bitcoin primarily serves as a digital currency, Ethereum is a platform that enables developers to build decentralized applications (DApps) on its blockchain. These applications can range from decentralized finance (DeFi) platforms to digital identity solutions.

3. Smart Contracts: Self-Executing Agreements

One of the most revolutionary aspects of Ethereum is the concept of smart contracts. These are self-executing contracts with the terms of the agreement directly written into code. They automatically execute when certain conditions are met, without the need for intermediaries.

4. Ether (ETH): The Fuel of Ethereum

Ether, often referred to as ETH, is the native cryptocurrency of the Ethereum network. It serves as the fuel that powers transactions, smart contracts, and interactions within the platform. Just as gas powers a car, ETH powers the Ethereum ecosystem.

5. Decentralized Applications (DApps)

Ethereum's platform has given rise to a multitude of DApps that offer various services and solutions. These DApps operate on a decentralized network, making them resistant to censorship and control by a single entity.

6. Decentralized Finance (DeFi)

DeFi is a hot topic in the Ethereum community. It refers to the use of blockchain and cryptocurrency technology to recreate traditional financial services without intermediaries. Lending, borrowing, trading, and yield farming are all part of the DeFi ecosystem on Ethereum.

7. Initial Coin Offerings (ICOs) and Tokenization

Ethereum facilitated the rise of Initial Coin Offerings (ICOs), a fundraising method where projects issue their own tokens on the Ethereum blockchain. This allowed startups to raise funds by offering investors these tokens, which represented a stake or utility in the project.

8. Ethereum's Upgrades: Hard Forks

Ethereum has undergone several upgrades to improve scalability, security, and functionality. These upgrades are often referred to as "hard forks." Notable hard forks include Byzantium, Constantinople, Istanbul, and Ethereum 2.0 (also known as Eth2 or Serenity).

9. Challenges and Scalability

While Ethereum has brought incredible innovation, it also faces challenges. One major challenge is scalability – the ability to handle many transactions quickly and efficiently. Ethereum's network congestion and high gas fees during periods of heavy usage have highlighted this issue.

10. Ethereum's Global Community

Ethereum has a vibrant and passionate global community of developers, enthusiasts, and advocates. This community collaborates on improving the platform, building applications, and discussing the future direction of Ethereum.

The Genesis of Ethereum: From Smart Contracts to Decentralized Applications

In our journey to understand Ethereum, let's delve deeper into its origins and the transformative features that have made it a powerhouse of innovation in the world of blockchain and cryptocurrencies.

1. Smart Contracts: The Building Blocks

At the heart of Ethereum's innovation are smart contracts. These are self-executing programs that automatically execute the terms of a contract when certain conditions are met. Imagine a contract that doesn't require intermediaries to enforce it; the code itself ensures compliance.

2. Decentralized Autonomous Organizations (DAOs)

Ethereum gave birth to the concept of Decentralized Autonomous Organizations (DAOs). These are organizations that operate based on smart contracts, allowing decisions to be made through consensus among participants rather than a centralized authority.

3. Turing Completeness: Limitless Possibilities

Unlike Bitcoin, which was designed for a specific purpose (peer-to-peer digital cash), Ethereum's programming language is Turing complete. This means it can perform any computation that can be expressed algorithmically. This flexibility enables the creation of DApps and complex smart contracts.

4. Initial Coin Offerings (ICOs)

Ethereum's capability to support custom tokens on its platform led to the rise of Initial Coin Offerings (ICOs). ICOs allowed startups to raise funds by issuing their own tokens on the Ethereum blockchain. While ICOs brought innovation, they also raised concerns about scams and regulatory challenges.

5. The DAO Hack and Ethereum Fork

Ethereum faced a major setback in 2016 with the infamous DAO hack. A vulnerability in the code of a major project led to a significant amount of Ether being stolen. To mitigate the impact, the Ethereum community conducted a contentious hard fork that led to the creation of two separate chains: Ethereum (ETH) and Ethereum Classic (ETC).

6. Ethereum Virtual Machine (EVM)

The Ethereum Virtual Machine is a decentralized computing environment that executes smart contracts. It ensures that all nodes on the Ethereum network interpret and execute the contracts in a consistent manner, maintaining the integrity of the blockchain.

7. The Rise of DApps

Ethereum's flexibility enabled the creation of a vast ecosystem of DApps. These applications span various industries, including finance, gaming, supply chain, identity, and more. Each DApp operates on the Ethereum blockchain, benefiting from its security and transparency.

8. Decentralized Finance (DeFi)

DeFi became one of the most transformative use cases for Ethereum. It encompasses various financial services, including lending, borrowing, trading, and yield farming, all operating on smart contracts. DeFi projects aim to recreate traditional financial systems without intermediaries.

9. Ethereum 2.0: The Upgrade

Ethereum 2.0, also known as Eth2 or Serenity, is a major upgrade that addresses Ethereum's scalability and energy consumption challenges. It introduces a transition from the current Proof of Work (PoW) consensus mechanism to Proof of Stake (PoS), which is expected to increase efficiency and reduce energy consumption.

10. Ethereal Innovations

Ethereum has sparked a wave of innovation and experimentation in the blockchain space. From creating new economic models to enabling secure digital identities, Ethereum's impact reaches far beyond cryptocurrency transactions.

Ethereum's Architecture: Unraveling the Building Blocks

Now that we've explored the origins and features of Ethereum, let's delve into the architecture that powers this groundbreaking platform. Understanding Ethereum's architecture will give us insight into how it operates and the technology behind its innovation.

1. Blockchain Basics

At the core of Ethereum is its blockchain, a distributed and immutable ledger that records all transactions and smart contracts. Each block contains a list of transactions, and once a block is added to the chain, it cannot be altered, ensuring transparency and security.

2. Nodes and Decentralization

Ethereum's network is made up of nodes, which are individual computers connected to the blockchain. Nodes validate transactions, maintain the network's security, and ensure consensus. The decentralized nature of these nodes makes Ethereum resistant to censorship and control.

3. Ethereum Clients

Ethereum has various software implementations, known as

clients, that run the Ethereum protocol. These clients, such as Geth and Parity, enable nodes to communicate and participate in the network. Users can choose which client they want to run, contributing to network diversity.

4. Gas and Transaction Fees

Transactions and smart contracts on Ethereum require computational resources. Gas is a measure of these resources, and users pay gas fees to incentivize miners to include their transactions in blocks. The more complex the operation, the more gas is required.

5. Smart Contracts and EVM

Smart contracts are the backbone of Ethereum's functionality. They are written in programming languages like Solidity and executed on the Ethereum Virtual Machine (EVM). The EVM ensures that smart contracts are executed consistently across all nodes, maintaining the integrity of the blockchain.

6. Decentralized Applications (DApps)

DApps are applications that operate on the Ethereum blockchain. They consist of a front-end interface and backend smart contracts. DApps can range from simple games to complex financial platforms, all interacting with the Ethereum network.

7. Interoperability and Ethereum Standards

Ethereum introduced the concept of standards like ERC-20 and ERC-721. ERC-20 tokens are fungible and can be used interchangeably, while ERC-721 tokens represent unique assets like digital collectibles. These standards enable interoperability between different DApps and platforms.

8. Ethereum Improvement Proposals (EIPs)

EIPs are proposals for changes and upgrades to the Ethereum network. They are discussed, debated, and implemented by the Ethereum community. EIPs have been responsible for introducing important features and improvements to the platform.

9. Privacy and Security

While Ethereum is transparent by design, privacy solutions have been developed to address confidentiality concerns. Zero-knowledge proofs and other cryptographic techniques are used to provide privacy for certain transactions and data.

10. Sharding and Ethereum 2.0

Ethereum's scalability issues have led to the development of Ethereum 2.0, which includes sharding. Sharding aims to divide the Ethereum network into smaller interconnected chains (shards), increasing its capacity to process transactions and smart contracts.

Ethereum's Impact: Revolutionizing Industries and Innovation

In this segment, we'll explore how Ethereum's innovative features have made a significant impact on various industries and paved the way for new forms of technology and collaboration.

1. Decentralized Finance (DeFi): Transforming Finance

Perhaps one of the most notable impacts of Ethereum is its role in the rise of decentralized finance (DeFi). DeFi platforms built on Ethereum enable users to lend, borrow, trade, and earn interest on their cryptocurrency holdings without relying on traditional financial intermediaries. This innovation has the potential to reshape the entire financial landscape, providing more accessible and open financial services.

2. Tokenization and Asset Ownership

Ethereum's ability to create custom tokens has led to the tokenization of real-world assets, such as real estate, art, and even ownership in companies. These digital tokens represent ownership and can be traded globally, enabling fractional ownership and democratizing investment opportunities.

3. Supply Chain Management

Blockchain technology, with Ethereum at the forefront, is transforming supply chain management. It allows for transparent and verifiable tracking of products at every stage, reducing fraud, ensuring authenticity, and enhancing consumer trust.

4. Digital Identity Solutions

Ethereum-based solutions are tackling identity management challenges. Self-sovereign digital identities, stored securely on the blockchain, empower individuals to control their personal data and share it only when necessary, potentially reducing identity theft and privacy violations.

5. Voting Systems and Governance

Governments and organizations are exploring Ethereum's potential for secure and transparent voting systems. Blockchain-based voting could enhance voter trust, prevent tampering, and streamline the election process.

6. Gaming and Non-Fungible Tokens (NFTs)

Ethereum has also revolutionized the gaming industry through the introduction of non-fungible tokens (NFTs). These unique digital assets represent ownership of in-game items, art, collectibles, and more. NFTs have created new avenues for artists and creators to monetize their digital creations.

7. Intellectual Property Protection

Smart contracts on Ethereum enable creators to prove ownership and manage intellectual property rights more efficiently.

Digital content creators can tokenize their work and establish automated payment systems for their creations.

8. Cross-Border Transactions and Remittances

Ethereum's global reach makes it an ideal platform for cross-border transactions and remittances. By bypassing traditional intermediaries, users can send funds across borders more quickly and at a lower cost.

9. Environmental and Social Impact

Ethereum is also being explored for its potential in creating positive social and environmental impact. Initiatives are emerging to leverage blockchain technology, including Ethereum, to address challenges like supply chain sustainability and charitable donations.

10. Challenges and Ongoing Development

While Ethereum's impact is vast, it also faces challenges. Scalability, energy consumption, and regulatory concerns are areas that the Ethereum community is actively addressing as the platform continues to evolve.

Ethereum's Future: Challenges, Upgrades, and Beyond

As we wrap up our exploration of Ethereum, let's take a closer look at what lies ahead for this groundbreaking platform. The journey of Ethereum is not only about its past and present impact but also about the exciting possibilities and challenges that await in the future.

1. Ethereum 2.0 and Proof of Stake

One of the most anticipated developments is Ethereum 2.0, a major upgrade aimed at addressing scalability and energy efficiency. Ethereum currently uses a Proof of Work (PoW) consensus mechanism, which requires significant energy consumption. Ethereum 2.0 will transition to Proof of Stake (PoS), where validators are chosen to create new blocks based on the amount of cryptocurrency, they "stake" as collateral. This change is expected to reduce energy consumption and increase transaction speed.

2. Sharding: Scaling the Network

Sharding is another critical upgrade under Ethereum 2.0. It involves breaking the blockchain into smaller interconnected chains called shards. Each shard can process transactions independently, significantly increasing the network's capacity and scalability.

3. Sustainability and Environmental Concerns

Ethereum's transition to PoS aims to address the environmental concerns associated with PoW. By consuming significantly less energy, Ethereum could become more environmentally friendly and align with sustainability goals.

4. Interoperability and Cross-Chain Solutions

Ethereum's success has spurred the development of other blockchains and platforms. Interoperability solutions are being explored to enable seamless communication and transactions between different blockchain networks, fostering collaboration and expanding possibilities.

5. Layer 2 Solutions

Layer 2 solutions are being developed to enhance Ethereum's scalability. These solutions operate "on top" of the main Ethereum blockchain, allowing for faster and cheaper transactions. The Lightning Network and state channels are examples of Layer 2 solutions.

6. Regulatory Challenges

As Ethereum and other blockchain technologies continue to evolve, they will likely face regulatory challenges. Governments and regulatory bodies are working to establish frameworks that balance innovation with consumer protection and financial integrity.

7. Continued Innovation

Ethereum's open-source nature encourages continuous

innovation. Developers around the world are working on new applications, protocols, and use cases that leverage the Ethereum platform.

8. Decentralization and Governance

As Ethereum grows, maintaining its decentralized nature and finding effective governance mechanisms will be essential. Balancing community-driven decision-making with the need for efficient upgrades is an ongoing challenge.

9. User Experience and Adoption

Improving user experience and making blockchain technology more accessible to the masses is crucial for widespread adoption. User-friendly wallets, intuitive interfaces, and education will play a vital role in Ethereum's journey to mainstream use.

10. Societal and Economic Impact

Ethereum's impact on society and the economy could be transformative. From enabling financial inclusion to reshaping industries, Ethereum has the potential to create positive change on a global scale.

Unveiling Binance Coin (BNB)

The Backbone of a Cryptocurrency Ecosystem

Imagine a coin that's not just used for buying and selling like regular money, but also plays a crucial role in powering an entire digital universe. This is Binance Coin (BNB), a cryptocurrency that's more than meets the eye. Let's dive into what BNB is all about and how it has become a cornerstone in the world of cryptocurrencies.

1. The Birth of Binance Coin

Binance Coin was created by one of the largest cryptocurrency exchanges in the world, Binance. It was launched through an Initial Coin Offering (ICO) in July 2017. Initially, BNB was built on the Ethereum blockchain, following the ERC-20 standard, but it later migrated to Binance's own blockchain called the Binance Chain.

2. The Utility of BNB

Unlike many cryptocurrencies that are primarily used for trading or investing, BNB serves a range of functions within the Binance ecosystem. It acts as a utility token, which means it has various practical uses beyond being a digital asset.

3. Trading Fee Discounts

One of the most notable uses of BNB is for trading fee discounts on the Binance platform. When users pay their trading fees using BNB, they receive a discount. This incentivizes traders to hold and use BNB, creating a strong demand for the token.

4. Token Burns

Binance periodically conducts what's known as a "token burn." This involves removing a certain number of BNB tokens from circulation, effectively reducing the total supply. Token burns are carried out to maintain the token's scarcity and potentially increase its value over time.

5. Launchpad for New Projects

Binance Launchpad is a platform that allows new cryptocurrency projects to raise funds through token sales. These token sales are usually conducted using BNB. This not only benefits the projects but also encourages users to acquire and hold BNB for potential participation in exciting new ventures.

6. Binance Smart Chain (BSC)

Binance Coin also plays a central role in the Binance Smart Chain, a blockchain that runs in parallel with the Binance Chain. BSC enables developers to create decentralized applications (DApps) and smart contracts, similar to Ethereum. BNB is used for transactions, smart contract execution, and as collateral in DeFi applications on the BSC.

7. DeFi and Yield Farming

Binance Coin's presence in the Binance Smart Chain has led to its involvement in the decentralized finance (DeFi) movement. DeFi platforms built on BSC use BNB for various purposes, including yield farming, where users provide liquidity to earn rewards.

8. The Rise of BNB's Value

Since its inception, Binance Coin's value has experienced significant growth. Factors contributing to its rise include its utility, regular token burns, and the overall growth of the Binance ecosystem.

9. Challenges and Developments

Despite its successes, Binance Coin also faces challenges. Competition in the cryptocurrency space is fierce, and BNB must continue to evolve to maintain its relevance. Binance is actively working on developing new features and use cases for BNB to ensure its long-term sustainability.

Binance Coin's Origins and Utility: Beyond a Standard Cryptocurrency

In the realm of cryptocurrencies, Binance Coin (BNB) stands out not only for its origins but also for its multifaceted utility. As we continue our exploration, let's dive deeper into how BNB's journey began and how its unique features set it apart from other digital currencies.

1. The Birth of BNB: From ICO to Mainstream

Binance Coin was born in 2017 through an Initial Coin Offering (ICO) held by Binance, a cryptocurrency exchange founded by Changpeng Zhao (CZ). During the ICO, investors could purchase BNB tokens, which were initially built on the Ethereum blockchain following the ERC-20 standard. This marked the inception of BNB's journey into the crypto world.

2. The Utility Token Paradigm

Unlike many cryptocurrencies that are primarily used for trading or investment, BNB was designed with utility in mind from the beginning. While it started to pay for trading fees on the Binance platform, its role has expanded to include a range of functions that contribute to the overall Binance ecosystem.

3. Fueling the Binance Ecosystem

BNB serves as the fuel that powers various aspects of the Binance ecosystem. Beyond trading fee discounts, BNB is used on the Binance Launchpad for token sales, providing users with the opportunity to invest in promising projects. This utilization not only benefits token buyers but also creates demand for BNB, influencing its value.

4. The Ingenious Token Burn Mechanism

Binance's commitment to maintaining the scarcity of BNB tokens is demonstrated through regular token burns. In these events, a portion of BNB tokens is permanently removed from circulation.

This intentional reduction in supply aims to counterbalance the creation of new tokens, potentially leading to appreciation in value over time.

5. Binance Smart Chain: A Game-Changer

The introduction of the Binance Smart Chain (BSC) further elevated BNB's utility. BSC serves as a parallel blockchain to the Binance Chain, enabling smart contract execution and decentralized applications. BNB is at the heart of BSC, facilitating transactions, powering smart contracts, and even playing a role in the booming world of decentralized finance (DeFi).

6. Bridging Traditional Finance and Cryptocurrency

Binance Coin's versatility extends beyond the crypto realm. Through strategic partnerships and integrations, BNB has found its way into traditional financial systems, allowing users to use BNB for payments, remittances, and even purchasing goods and services.

7. Challenges and Evolution

While BNB has achieved remarkable success, challenges persist. The evolving landscape of cryptocurrencies demands continuous innovation. Binance recognizes this and is committed to adapting BNB to meet the changing needs of users and the industry.

8. The Community's Role

BNB's journey would be incomplete without the vibrant community that supports and utilizes it. The Binance community, along with the developers and visionaries behind the project, continues to shape the trajectory of BNB's evolution.

The Many Faces of BNB: Use Cases and Innovations on the Binance Smart Chain

Beyond being a mere cryptocurrency, Binance Coin (BNB) has evolved into a versatile digital asset with a multitude of uses, especially within the Binance Smart Chain (BSC) ecosystem. In this section, we'll delve into the various roles BNB plays and the innovations it has spurred on the BSC platform.

1. Transaction Fuel and Network Fees

One of the core functions of BNB within the Binance ecosystem is its role as "gas" for transactions. Whenever users conduct transactions on the Binance Smart Chain—whether they're sending tokens or interacting with decentralized applications (DApps)—they pay a small amount of BNB as a network fee. This fee helps incentivize miners and validators to process and validate transactions.

2. Decentralized Applications (DApps)

The Binance Smart Chain hosts a variety of DApps that leverage BNB's capabilities. These applications span a wide range of sectors, from decentralized finance (DeFi) platforms offering lending and yield farming to decentralized exchanges (DEXs) where users can trade cryptocurrencies directly without intermediaries.

3. BNB as Collateral in DeFi

Decentralized finance is one of the fastest-growing sectors in the crypto world, and BNB plays a pivotal role here too. In DeFi platforms built on BSC, users can lock up their BNB as collateral to borrow other cryptocurrencies. This system allows users to access liquidity without the need for traditional financial institutions.

4. Yield Farming and Staking

Yield farming involves users providing liquidity to DeFi platforms in exchange for rewards. BNB holders can participate in yield farming by supplying BNB to liquidity pools, earning a share of transaction fees and additional tokens as rewards. Staking, on the other hand, involves locking up BNB to support the network's operations and security, with stakers receiving rewards in return.

5. NFTs and BNB

The non-fungible token (NFT) craze has also found its way to Binance Smart Chain. BNB serves as a key currency in NFT marketplaces and platforms where users can buy, sell, and trade unique digital collectibles, art, and virtual items.

6. Token Swaps and Cross-Chain Solutions

BNB's utility extends beyond the Binance Smart Chain. It's also used as a bridge asset for cross-chain swaps, allowing users to easily exchange their BNB for tokens on other blockchains. This enhances liquidity and accessibility for users across different blockchain networks.

7. Gaming and Virtual Economies

The Binance Smart Chain has seen the emergence of blockchain-based games that utilize BNB as an in-game currency. These games often incorporate decentralized ownership of in-game assets, enabling players to truly own their virtual belongings.

8. Sustainable Growth

As Binance Coin's utility continues to expand, its ecosystem attracts more users, developers, and projects. This growth further fuels demand for BNB and promotes the development of innovative use cases.

9. Community Involvement

The BNB community, comprising traders, investors, developers, and enthusiasts, plays an essential role in shaping its trajectory. Community-driven initiatives and engagement foster a collaborative ecosystem that contributes to BNB's ongoing success.

Binance Coin's Future: Challenges, Developments, and Impact on the Crypto Landscape

As we journey through the world of Binance Coin (BNB), we must also look ahead to its future. The path BNB takes will not only shape its own destiny but also have ripple effects throughout the broader cryptocurrency landscape. In this section, we'll explore the challenges BNB may face, ongoing developments, and its potential impact on the ever-evolving crypto realm.

1. Sustaining Momentum

One of the key challenges BNB faces is sustaining the momentum it has gained over the years. The cryptocurrency industry is highly dynamic, with new projects and technologies emerging constantly. To remain relevant, BNB needs to continue offering innovative solutions and use cases that cater to changing user demands.

2. Competition in DeFi and Beyond

As Binance Coin expands its reach into decentralized finance (DeFi) and various other sectors, it encounters competition from other cryptocurrencies and platforms. Other utility tokens and blockchain networks are vying for similar roles, so BNB must continue to differentiate itself and offer unique value propositions.

3. Regulatory Landscape

The regulatory environment for cryptocurrencies is evolving, and BNB, like other digital assets, may be affected by regulatory changes. Navigating the regulatory landscape while ensuring user privacy, security, and compliance will be a delicate balance that Binance and BNB holders must maintain.

4. Technological Upgrades

To meet the demands of scalability, security, and user experience, Binance Coin will likely undergo technological upgrades. Whether through blockchain enhancements, consensus mechanism changes, or interoperability solutions, these upgrades will play a pivotal role in BNB's future growth.

5. Expanding Ecosystem

The Binance ecosystem continues to expand beyond just cryptocurrency trading. Binance's ventures into decentralized finance, non-fungible tokens, blockchain-based games, and more provide opportunities for BNB to be integrated into diverse use cases.

6. User Experience and Accessibility

Enhancing the user experience is paramount for mass adoption. BNB's continued efforts to improve wallet interfaces, transaction speed, and ease of use will contribute to its widespread acceptance.

7. Global Impact

As a leading cryptocurrency exchange, Binance and its native token BNB have a global footprint. The impact of BNB's innovations and utility can extend beyond the borders of its home country, influencing how people interact with digital assets around the world.

8. Collaboration and Partnerships

Collaboration with other blockchain projects, enterprises, and institutions can further propel BNB's adoption. Strategic partnerships can open up new avenues for BNB's utility and reach.

9. Community and Decentralization

BNB's community is a driving force behind its growth. Balancing community-driven decisions with efficient governance structures will be crucial for maintaining decentralization while fostering progress.

10. Shaping the Landscape

Binance Coin's trajectory doesn't just affect its own ecosystem—it contributes to shaping the entire cryptocurrency landscape. The innovations, challenges, and solutions that BNB experiences will inspire other projects and contribute to the industry's collective growth.

CHAPTER 6 WHAT IS DEFI?

Decentralized Finance, or DeFi, is a groundbreaking concept that has the potential to revolutionize the world of finance. In simple terms, it refers to a new way of handling money and financial services without relying on traditional banks or intermediaries. It's like digital finance but on a whole new level! Imagine a world where you can lend money, borrow funds, trade assets, and even earn interest on your savings directly from your smartphone or computer, all without going through a bank. That's what DeFi is all about!

At its core, DeFi is based on blockchain technology, which is a secure and transparent way to keep track of transactions and agreements. Unlike regular banks that keep all your data and control your money, DeFi platforms run on a decentralized network, where no single entity has complete power. Instead, it's like a community of people coming together to manage and use their money more efficiently.

The idea of DeFi started gaining popularity around 2017 and

has been growing ever since. It all began with the invention of Bitcoin, the first cryptocurrency, which showed the world how digital money could work without banks. People realized that they could create financial systems that were fairer, more open, and accessible to everyone, no matter where they lived.

As more people got interested in cryptocurrencies, developers started building new DeFi platforms and applications. One of the most important breakthroughs was the introduction of smart contracts. These are like self-executing agreements written in code, which means once certain conditions are met, they automatically carry out the terms of the agreement. Smart contracts made it possible to create complex financial services without relying on banks or middlemen.

Key Principles and Advantages of DeFi

Defi is built on some essential principles that make it so exciting and promising:

1. **Transparency:** All transactions on DeFi platforms are recorded on a public blockchain, making them visible to everyone. This transparency helps build trust and ensures that nobody can cheat the system. Anyone can verify transactions and track where the money is flowing.

2. **Accessibility:** One of the most significant advantages of DeFi is that anyone with an internet connection can access these

services. This is a game-changer for people who don't have access to traditional banking services due to geographical or economic reasons. As long as you have a smartphone or a computer, you can participate in the DeFi ecosystem.

3. **Security:** DeFi platforms use strong encryption and decentralization, making them more secure against hacks and cyber-attacks compared to centralized systems. Since data is distributed across a network of computers, it becomes challenging for malicious actors to manipulate the system or compromise sensitive information.

4. **Financial Inclusion:** DeFi has the potential to bring financial services to billions of people who are currently excluded from the traditional financial system, especially in developing countries. For many, DeFi might be the first exposure to formal financial services, allowing them to participate in the global economy and improve their livelihoods.

5. **Control over Assets:** With DeFi, you have full control over your assets, like cryptocurrencies. No bank or government can freeze your account or take away your money without your permission. You become the sole custodian of your funds, reducing the risk of unauthorized access and asset seizure.

6. **Earning Passive Income:** In DeFi, you can put your money to work and earn interest or rewards for providing liquidity to the system. Instead of leaving your savings in a traditional bank with minimal interest, you can earn higher returns by participating in lending or liquidity provision pools.

DeFi is still a relatively new concept, and it's constantly evolving with new ideas and technologies. As it grows, it's crucial to be aware of the risks and challenges it might face, such as smart contract vulnerabilities and regulatory uncertainties. However, despite these challenges, DeFi holds great promise for shaping the future of finance in a more inclusive and decentralized way.

Defi Components and Ecosystem: Unlocking the Power of Digital Finance

Understanding DeFi Protocols and Smart Contracts

In the world of DeFi, protocols, and smart contracts play a crucial role in enabling various financial services without relying on traditional intermediaries. A protocol is like a set of rules that define how different DeFi applications and platforms work. These protocols are often open source, meaning anyone can access and review the code, ensuring transparency and security.

One of the most significant breakthroughs in DeFi is the introduction of smart contracts. Think of smart contracts as digital agreements that automatically execute themselves when specific conditions are met. They are built on blockchain technology, making them secure and tamper-proof. For example, a smart contract could be used to facilitate a loan between two people: once the borrower repays the loan amount with interest, the smart contract automatically releases the funds to the lender.

DeFi Lending and Borrowing Platforms

DeFi lending and borrowing platforms have emerged as a popular and essential part of the DeFi ecosystem. These platforms allow users to lend out their digital assets and earn interest or borrow assets by collateralizing their holdings. It's like putting your money to work while helping others in need.

To lend on a DeFi platform, you simply deposit your assets into a smart contract, and the platform lends them out to borrowers. In return, you receive interest on your deposit. The interest rates are often determined by supply and demand dynamics, with higher demand for borrowing leading to higher interest rates for lenders.

On the other hand, borrowers can use DeFi lending platforms to obtain loans without having to go through the hassle of traditional banks. They need to provide collateral, usually in the form of other digital assets, which they get back once the loan is repaid. This collateral minimizes the risk for lenders and ensures that the loan is backed by real value.

Decentralized Exchanges (DEXs) and Automated Market Makers (AMMs)

Decentralized exchanges, or DEXs, are another essential component of DeFi. These exchanges allow users to trade digital assets directly with one another without the need for centralized authority. In a DEX, you have full control over your assets, and you don't need to deposit them into a centralized exchange wallet.

Automated Market Makers, or AMMs, are a specific type of DEX that uses smart contracts to determine asset prices and facilitate trades. Instead of relying on order books like traditional exchanges, AMMs use liquidity pools to provide liquidity for trading pairs. Users can contribute their assets to these pools and earn rewards in return. When you want to trade, the AMM automatically matches your trade with the pool's liquidity.

Yield Farming and Liquidity Provision in DeFi

Yield farming is an exciting concept in DeFi that allows users to earn rewards by providing liquidity to DeFi protocols. When you contribute your assets to a liquidity pool, you receive tokens representing your share of the pool. These tokens can then be used to participate in other DeFi protocols, effectively farming for rewards.

Liquidity provision is crucial for the smooth functioning of DeFi platforms, especially decentralized exchanges and AMMs. By providing liquidity, users help ensure that there are enough assets available for trading, reducing slippage and improving the overall user experience.

In conclusion, DeFi protocols and applications have opened up a world of possibilities in the realm of digital finance. With smart contracts, lending and borrowing platforms, decentralized exchanges, and yield farming, DeFi is empowering individuals with greater financial control and opportunities. However, as the DeFi ecosystem grows, it's essential for users to be cautious and understand the risks associated with using these platforms.

Challenges and Risks in DeFi: Navigating the World of Digital Finance

Security Concerns and Vulnerabilities

While DeFi offers exciting opportunities, it's not without its challenges. One of the most significant concerns in the world of DeFi is security. DeFi platforms and smart contracts are built on blockchain technology, which is secure and transparent. However, smart contracts are not immune to vulnerabilities.

Smart contract bugs or coding errors can lead to serious consequences. In the past, we've seen incidents where hackers exploited these vulnerabilities to steal millions of dollars from DeFi platforms. To mitigate these risks, developers and users must be cautious and thoroughly audit smart contracts before deploying them on the blockchain.

Regulatory and Compliance Challenges

The decentralized and borderless nature of DeFi raises questions about regulations and compliance. Traditional financial systems are heavily regulated to ensure consumer protection and financial stability. However, DeFi operates beyond national boundaries and often without intermediaries, making it challenging for regulators to oversee and enforce rules.

As governments and regulatory bodies catch up with this new technology, there could be changes in regulations that impact the DeFi landscape. DeFi projects and users must stay informed about evolving regulations to ensure compliance and avoid potential legal risks.

Scalability and Interoperability Issues

Blockchain technology, while innovative, faces scalability and interoperability challenges. As the number of users and transactions on DeFi platforms grows, it puts a strain on the blockchain network, leading to slower transaction times and higher fees. This can limit the adoption of DeFi by mainstream users.

Interoperability is another concern. Different DeFi platforms may use different blockchains, making it difficult for them to communicate and share data seamlessly. Achieving cross-chain interoperability is essential for the growth and efficiency of the DeFi ecosystem.

User Education and Phishing Attacks

DeFi is still relatively new, and many users may not fully understand how it works. Lack of proper education can lead to mistakes like entering incorrect wallet addresses or falling victim to phishing attacks. Phishing attacks are when scammers trick users into giving away their private keys or passwords, leading to the loss of their funds.

It's crucial for users to educate themselves about the basics of DeFi, secure practices, and how to identify potential scams. Being vigilant and double-checking transactions can help protect against phishing attacks.

Risks of over-collateralization and Liquidation

In DeFi lending, borrowers are required to provide collateral to secure their loans. While this reduces the risk for lenders, it can lead to over-collateralization, where borrowers need to deposit more assets than the loan's value. If the collateral's value drops significantly, borrowers may face liquidation, where their collateral is sold off to cover the outstanding loan amount. This can result in the loss of assets for borrowers.

Users need to carefully assess the risks involved and avoid overleveraging their assets to protect themselves from potential liquidations.

In conclusion, while DeFi presents an exciting new frontier in finance, it comes with its fair share of challenges and risks. Addressing security concerns, staying informed about regulations, improving scalability and interoperability, educating users, and managing risks are crucial for the sustainable growth of DeFi.

Real-World Use Cases and Adoption: Embracing the Power of DeFi

DeFi Applications in Traditional Finance

DeFi is not just an isolated bubble; it has the potential to impact traditional finance positively. One of the most exciting use cases of DeFi in traditional finance is cross-border remittances. Sending money across borders can be expensive and time-consuming, but with DeFi, it becomes faster and more affordable. Blockchain-based remittance platforms can enable instant transfers with lower fees, benefiting both senders and receivers.

Moreover, DeFi can improve financial inclusion by providing banking services to the unbanked and underbanked populations. With just a smartphone and internet access, people in remote areas can access DeFi applications, such as savings, lending, and insurance, bringing them into the formal financial system.

DeFi in Emerging Markets and Financial Inclusion

Emerging markets, with their unique financial challenges, stand to gain significantly from DeFi adoption. In many developing countries, access to traditional banking services is limited, and people often rely on informal lending systems with high interest rates. DeFi can disrupt this status quo by offering alternative financial services, reducing costs, and providing more accessible options.

Moreover, DeFi can enable micro-lending, allowing individuals to lend small amounts of money to entrepreneurs and small businesses. This facilitates economic growth in underserved areas and empowers local communities to take control of their financial futures.

DeFi's Impact on Investment and Wealth Management

DeFi also opens up new avenues for investment and wealth management. With traditional investments, individuals often rely on intermediaries like brokers, who charge high fees. DeFi's decentralized nature removes the need for middlemen, reducing costs and increasing transparency.

DeFi protocols offer a wide range of investment opportunities, from traditional assets like stocks and bonds to novel concepts like tokenized real estate and art. This diversity allows investors to build more diversified portfolios and access assets that were previously out of reach.

DeFi Adoption and Future Growth Prospects

The adoption of DeFi has been steadily growing, but it's still in its early stages. As more people become familiar with cryptocurrencies and blockchain technology, the user base for DeFi applications is expected to expand rapidly.

Institutions and companies are also showing increasing interest in DeFi. Traditional financial institutions are exploring ways to integrate DeFi into their existing services, seeking to tap into the benefits of decentralization and cost-effectiveness.

However, for DeFi to achieve mainstream adoption, several challenges must be addressed. User education remains a priority, as many potential users are still unfamiliar with cryptocurrencies and DeFi concepts. Moreover, regulatory clarity is crucial to ensure that DeFi platforms comply with relevant laws and regulations without stifling innovation.

DeFi: A Journey into the Future of Finance

DeFi represents a paradigm shift in the world of finance, offering innovative solutions that empower individuals and promote financial inclusion. It presents a decentralized, transparent, and accessible alternative to traditional finance, with the potential to revolutionize the global financial landscape.

As we embark on this exciting journey into the future of finance, it's essential for users, developers, and regulators to work together to overcome challenges and seize opportunities. By harnessing the power of DeFi responsibly and collaboratively, we can create a financial system that truly belongs to the people

What the Internet Computer (ICP) Crypto is?

The Internet Computer is a special kind of computer system that's really good at handling transactions and programs on the Internet. It's different from regular computers because it's super-fast and can do lots of different tasks, like managing money, digital art, online games, and much more.

At the core of the Internet Computer is the ICP token. Think of it like a special digital coin that has two jobs: one, it's used to pay for things like using the computer, and two, it helps make decisions about how the computer works. People who use the computer can earn ICP tokens as rewards for helping it run smoothly.

The Internet Computer project was started by the DFINITY Foundation to make the Internet more secure and open for everyone. They want to create a place where billions of people can do things online, like using apps and sharing content, without relying on big companies.

What makes the Internet Computer cool is that it's super-fast, making it possible to use apps and do things on the Internet in real-time. It can grow and handle lots of users without slowing down or losing its reliability.

Here's how it all works:

- The Internet Computer is controlled by something called the Network Nervous System (NNS), which is like a big, smart brain.

People who use the computer can suggest changes and ideas to the NNS, and everyone gets to vote on them. If you own ICP tokens, you can participate in these decisions.

- The heart of the computer is made up of small programs called Canisters. These programs are super secure and independent, which is important for keeping everything safe and running smoothly. Apps use these Canisters to do their jobs.

- The DFINITY Foundation, which created the Internet Computer, also built a system for creating secure identities on the Internet. This means you can use the computer without worrying too much about your privacy and security.

In short, the Internet Computer is like a powerful, fast, and open computer for the Internet, and it's run by a smart system that listens to the people who use it. It's changing the way we use the internet, making it more secure, open, and efficient for everyone.

What Uniswap (UNI) Crypto is?

Uniswap is like a big, open marketplace for trading digital currencies. It's different from regular stock exchanges because it doesn't rely on big companies to make trades happen. Instead, it uses smart computer programs to handle everything.

UNI is the special token that's used on Uniswap. Think of it as a voting coin – people who own UNI tokens get to help decide how

Uniswap works and can make proposals for changes.

Uniswap is a big network that connects lots of different apps, developers, traders, and people who put their money into the system. It started on Ethereum but now works on other systems like Polygon, Optimism, and Arbitrum.

Uniswap is a super popular way to trade digital tokens. It doesn't need a middleman to make trades happen – it uses smart programs to do that. These programs also create pools of digital tokens to make trading easier.

Here's how it all works:

• You can go to the Uniswap platform to trade digital tokens directly with other people, without needing a company in the middle.

• Uniswap is secure and doesn't rely on a single company to run it. You have control over your own tokens and transactions.

• The people who created Uniswap are always working to make it better. They have a special token, UNI, that lets users vote on changes and improvements.

Uniswap is a cool way to trade digital tokens without needing a big company, and it's powered by smart programs that make trading easy and secure. It's like a big marketplace for the digital currency world!

What Chainlink (LINK) is?

Chainlink is like the bridge between the regular internet and the world of cryptocurrencies. It helps connect data from the real world (like weather, prices, and other information) to cryptocurrencies and the applications that run on them. LINK is the special token that's used on Chainlink. Think of it as a reward coin - people who help provide accurate data to the network can earn LINK tokens.

Chainlink's technology is super important for apps that use cryptocurrencies, like those in the DeFi world, gaming, and NFTs. It uses smart contracts to make sure that the data it provides is reliable and can be trusted.

Here's how it all works:

- Chainlink has a network of computers, called nodes or oracles, that collect real-world data and turn it into a format that apps on the blockchain can understand.

- Apps that run on the blockchain, like DeFi apps, need this real-world data to work properly. Chainlink connects these apps to the data they need.

- People and companies that provide data to Chainlink can earn LINK tokens as a reward.

- LINK tokens are also used to pay for the services on Chainlink, like getting data. This helps keep the network running smoothly.

- Chainlink's technology makes sure the data is trustworthy, which is crucial for apps that rely on it.

Chainlink is a key part of the cryptocurrency world, making it possible for apps to use real-world data in a secure and reliable way. It's used in many different applications and is an important part of the crypto ecosystem

CHAPTER 7 WHAT IS A BULL OR BEAR MARKET FOR CRYPTOCURRENCIES?

A bull market and a bear market are terms used to describe the overall direction of the prices in a financial market, including the world of cryptocurrencies. Understanding these terms can help you make sense of how the value of cryptocurrencies changes over time.

Bull Market: A bull market is a term used to describe a market where prices are rising or expected to rise. It's like when a bull charges forward with its horns up. In the context of cryptocurrencies, a bull market means that the overall sentiment and confidence among investors are positive, and they are optimistic about the future of the market. During a bull market, there's a lot of buying activity, which drives the prices higher.

In a bull market, you'll often see a series of upward price movements, where cryptocurrencies reach new all-time highs or significant milestones. Many people are excited about the potential for profits, and it may seem like everyone is talking about cryptocurrencies and investing in them.

Bear Market:: On the other hand, a bear market is a market where prices are falling or expected to fall. It's like when a bear swipes its paws down. In a bear market for cryptocurrencies, investor sentiment is pessimistic, and people are cautious or even fearful about the future of the market. During a bear market, there's a lot of selling activity, which pushes the prices lower.

In a bear market, prices can experience prolonged declines, and cryptocurrencies may lose significant value compared to their previous highs. This can be discouraging for investors, and many people may start to lose interest in cryptocurrencies or even sell their holdings to avoid further losses.

Understanding Market Trends and Their Impact on Cryptocurrencies

Market trends are patterns or movements in the prices of cryptocurrencies that repeat over time. These trends can be influenced by various factors, including news events, technological advancements, market sentiment, and economic conditions. Understanding market trends can help you make informed decisions when investing in cryptocurrencies.

Trend Lines: Trend lines are used to identify the general direction of the market. An upward-sloping trend line indicates a bull market, while a downward-sloping trend line indicates a bear market. Identifying these trends can help you determine the overall sentiment in the market.

Support and Resistance Levels: Support levels are price points where a cryptocurrency's price tends to stop falling, while resistance levels are price points where it tends to stop rising. These levels can act as barriers to further price movements and provide insights into potential buying or selling opportunities.

Volatility: Cryptocurrency markets are known for their high volatility, which means that prices can change rapidly in a short period. Volatility can be both an opportunity and a risk. It offers the potential for significant profits during bull markets but can lead to substantial losses during bear markets.

Strategies for Navigating Bull and Bear Markets

Navigating bull and bear markets requires a thoughtful approach and risk management. Here are some strategies to consider:

- **Diversification**: Diversifying your cryptocurrency portfolio can help spread risk. Invest in a mix of different cryptocurrencies rather than putting all your money into one. This way, if one cryptocurrency's value drops significantly, the others might help balance out the losses.

- **Long-term vs. Short-term Investing:** Decide on your investment horizon. Long-term investors believe in the potential of cryptocurrencies and are willing to hold onto their investments for extended periods, even during bear markets. Short-term traders, on the other hand, take advantage of price fluctuations and may buy and sell more frequently.

- **Risk Management:** Only invest money that you can afford to lose. Cryptocurrency markets can be highly unpredictable, so it's essential to have a clear risk management strategy in place to protect your investments.

- **Research and Education**: Stay informed about the latest developments in the cryptocurrency space. Knowledge about the projects you invest in can help you make more informed decisions.

In conclusion, understanding bull and bear markets is essential for anyone interested in the world of cryptocurrencies. By recognizing market trends and implementing strategies for navigating different market conditions, you can make more informed decisions and potentially maximize your gains while minimizing your risks. However, remember that investing in cryptocurrencies carries inherent risks, and it's crucial to do your research and invest responsibly.

"MOBILE WAS INTERNET 2.0.
IT CHANGED EVERYTHING.
CRYPTO IS INTERNET 3.0."

GIL PENCHINA

CHAPTER 8 WHAT IS CRYPTOGRAPHY?

Imagine you have a secret message that you want to share with a friend. However, you don't want anyone else to read it. That's where cryptography comes in! Cryptography is like a magic code that turns your message into a secret code, known as ciphertext, making it unreadable to anyone who doesn't have the key to unlock it.

In simple terms, cryptography is the art of securing digital assets, messages, and communications by converting them into a secret code using mathematical algorithms. It's like putting your information inside a virtual safe, protected from prying eyes.

The Art of Securing Digital Assets with Cryptography:

In today's digital world, where information is shared online, cybersecurity is of utmost importance. Cryptography plays a crucial role in protecting sensitive data, such as passwords, financial transactions, and personal information, from unauthorized access and potential hackers.

There are two primary types of cryptographic techniques used in securing digital assets:

Symmetric Encryption: In symmetric encryption, the same key is used for both encryption and decryption. It's like having a secret key that both you and your friend use to lock and unlock the message. While this method is straightforward and fast, there is a challenge with securely sharing the secret key. If someone else intercepts the key, they can read your encrypted message. To address this issue, secure key exchange methods are used to transmit the key securely between parties without revealing it to potential eavesdroppers. Common symmetric encryption algorithms include Advanced Encryption Standard (AES) and Data Encryption Standard (DES).

Asymmetric Encryption (Public-Key Cryptography) Asymmetric encryption uses two different keys - a public key and a private key. The public key is used for encryption, and anyone can access it. It's like having a mailbox where anyone can drop letters, but only you have the private key to open and read the messages.

The private key is kept secret and is used for decryption. This way, even if someone knows the public key, they won't be able to read the encrypted messages without the private key. Asymmetric encryption is widely used for secure communication and digital signatures in cryptocurrencies and online transactions. Common asymmetric encryption algorithms include RSA (Rivest-Shamir-Adleman) and ECC (Elliptic Curve Cryptography).

Cryptographic Techniques Used in Cryptocurrencies

Cryptocurrencies heavily rely on cryptography to secure digital assets and enable secure transactions on blockchain networks. Here are some cryptographic techniques used in cryptocurrencies:

- **Hash Functions**: Hash functions are algorithms that convert any input data into a fixed-size string of characters. This output is called the hash or message digest. The hash is unique to the input data and acts as a digital fingerprint. It's used to verify the integrity of data and ensure that transactions on the blockchain are valid. Common cryptographic hash functions used in cryptocurrencies include SHA-256 (Bitcoin) and Keccak-256 (Ethereum).

- **Digital Signatures:** Digital signatures are used to prove the authenticity and integrity of a message or transaction. They are created using the private key of the sender and verified using the sender's public key. Digital signatures ensure that transactions are not tampered with and that they come from the correct sender.

- **Elliptic Curve Cryptography (ECC):** ECC is an asymmetric encryption technique widely used in cryptocurrencies due to its efficiency and strong security. It allows for shorter key sizes compared to traditional asymmetric encryption algorithms while providing the same level of security.

"NOT UNDERSTANDING BLOCKCHAIN. IT'S GOING TO SMACK YOU DOWN AND MAKE YOU BLEED."

MARK CUBAN

CHAPTER 9 WHAT IS NFT?

Unraveling Non-Fungible Tokens and Their Unique Properties

In the exciting world of cryptocurrencies and blockchain technology, you may have come across a buzzword called Non-Fungible Tokens (NFTs). But what exactly are NFTs, and why are they gaining so much attention? Let's unravel the mystery of NFTs and explore their unique properties.

What are Non-Fungible Tokens (NFTs)?

At its core, a Non-Fungible Token (NFT) is a digital asset that represents ownership of a unique item or piece of content on a blockchain. While cryptocurrencies like Bitcoin and Ethereum are fungible, meaning one unit can be exchanged for another identical unit, NFTs are non-fungible, which means each token has a distinct value and cannot be exchanged on a one-to-one basis.

Understanding the Difference between Fungible and Non-Fungible Assets

To better grasp the concept of NFTs, let's imagine a simple comparison. Fungible assets are like dollar bills – each dollar bill is interchangeable with another, and the value remains the same. For example, if you lend a friend $5 and they later return the same amount, you wouldn't mind if they gave you a different $5 bill in return.

On the other hand, non-fungible assets are like unique paintings or rare collectible cards. Each painting or card has its own distinct value, and you would not exchange one for another because each holds its own special significance. Similarly, NFTs represent unique digital items like art, music, videos, virtual real estate, and other digital collectibles, making them inherently different from one another.

The Role of Blockchain Technology in NFTs

NFTs rely on blockchain technology to function. A blockchain is a decentralized and transparent digital ledger that records transactions across a network of computers. In the case of NFTs, information about the digital asset and its ownership is stored securely on the blockchain.

Blockchain technology ensures the authenticity, scarcity, and immutability of NFTs. Once an NFT is created, its ownership history and metadata are permanently recorded on the blockchain, making it tamper-proof and verifiable.

NFTs and Ownership: Tokenizing Digital and Physical Assets

One of the most revolutionary aspects of NFTs is their ability to tokenize digital and physical assets. Tokenization is the process of converting an asset into a digital token, and NFTs make it possible to represent ownership of both intangible and tangible items on the blockchain.

For digital artists, musicians, and content creators, NFTs offer a new way to monetize their work and maintain control over their intellectual property. By tokenizing their creations as NFTs, artists can sell them directly to collectors, bypassing traditional intermediaries and ensuring they receive a fair share of the profits.

Moreover, NFTs have extended their reach beyond the digital realm. They can also represent ownership of physical assets like real estate, luxury goods, and even legal documents. Through tokenization, these physical assets can become more easily tradable and accessible to a global audience.

The Importance of Scarcity and Rarity in NFTs

Scarcity and rarity play a crucial role in the value of NFTs. Just like in the physical world, items that are scarce and rare tend to hold higher value in the NFT market. Collectors and enthusiasts are often willing to pay a premium for exclusive and limited-edition NFTs, creating a market for digital art and collectibles.

Creators can leverage this aspect to design unique collections, limited editions, and one-of-a-kind pieces to attract buyers and collectors. NFT platforms and marketplaces often feature auctions and bidding mechanisms, driving up the price for highly sought-after NFTs.

Real-World Use Cases and the NFT Market Boom

Now that we have a better understanding of what Non-Fungible Tokens (NFTs) are, let's dive into their real-world applications and the booming NFT market.

Exploring NFT Use Cases Beyond Art: Gaming, Collectibles, and Virtual Real Estate

While NFTs initially gained popularity in the art world, their use cases have expanded far beyond that. In the gaming industry, NFTs are revolutionizing the concept of digital ownership. Players can now own and trade in-game assets like characters, skins, weapons, and virtual real estate as NFTs. This ownership enables players to truly own and control their digital belongings, even outside the game's ecosystem.

NFT collectibles are another exciting use case. Remember the thrill of collecting trading cards or rare toys? NFTs have brought that joy into the digital realm, where unique digital collectibles can be bought, sold, and displayed in virtual galleries or social platforms. These digital collectibles can hold both sentimental and financial value for collectors.

Virtual real estate is a novel NFT use case, where digital plots of land or virtual properties are tokenized on the blockchain. These

NFTs enable users to own, trade, and develop virtual spaces within virtual worlds and metaverses. Virtual real estate has become a hot market, attracting investors and developers eager to explore the potential of immersive digital experiences.

NFTs in the Music Industry: Transforming Music Ownership and Royalties

For musicians and artists, NFTs offer new avenues for creativity, ownership, and revenue generation. Musicians can tokenize their music, albums, concert tickets, and exclusive experiences as NFTs. Fans can purchase these NFTs, becoming not just passive listeners but active stakeholders in the artist's journey.

NFTs also have the potential to revolutionize the music industry's royalty system. Through smart contracts, artists can receive a direct share of the revenue whenever their NFTs are sold or resold. This ensures that artists continue to benefit from their work, even after the initial sale.

Sports and NFTs: Tokenizing Athlete Memorabilia and Fan Engagement

In the sports world, NFTs have opened new opportunities for athletes, teams, and fans alike. Athlete memorabilia, such as game-worn jerseys, autographed merchandise, and limited-edition collectibles, can be tokenized as NFTs. Fans can own these digital representations of sports history, forging a deeper connection with their favorite athletes and teams.

NFTs also enhance fan engagement by offering exclusive experiences and rewards. Sports organizations can create unique fan experiences, like virtual meet-and-greets or access to exclusive content, as NFTs. These experiences become treasured souvenirs for fans, fostering a stronger sense of community and loyalty.

NFTs in the Real Estate Sector: Fractional Ownership and Digital Land

The real estate industry is also embracing NFTs, enabling fractional ownership of properties. NFTs allow investors to own a percentage of a property, making real estate investment more accessible and liquid. Fractional ownership NFTs can be traded on secondary markets, creating a new avenue for property investment and diversification.

Virtual real estate, as mentioned earlier, is also gaining traction. NFTs represent digital plots of land within virtual worlds and metaverses. As these virtual spaces become more immersive and attractive, the demand for virtual real estate NFTs is on the rise.

NFT Market Trends and the Surge in Popularity: Understanding the NFT Craze

The NFT market has experienced a significant surge in popularity, attracting attention from artists, investors, celebrities, and enthusiasts alike. The unique properties of NFTs, such as ownership, provenance, and scarcity, have contributed to their appeal.

NFT marketplaces, platforms, and auction houses have sprung up, facilitating the buying, selling, and trading of NFTs. Some of the most prominent NFT marketplaces include OpenSea, Rarible, and SuperRare.

While the NFT market presents exciting opportunities, it also faces challenges such as scalability, environmental concerns related to energy usage, and issues of copyright and intellectual property. As the market continues to evolve, addressing these challenges will be crucial for its sustainable growth.

NFT Examples and High-Profile Sales

Let's dive deeper into the world of Non-Fungible Tokens (NFTs) and explore some exciting examples of NFTs and high-profile sales that have captured the attention of the world.

Iconic NFT Artworks: A Look at Pioneering NFT Artists and Their Impact

NFTs have provided artists with a new way to showcase their work and connect with their audience. Some of the most iconic NFT artworks have become digital sensations, fetching millions of dollars in the NFT market.

For instance, the artist Beeple made headlines with his NFT artwork "Everyday: The First 5000 Days," a collection of 5,000 digital images created every day over 13 years. The artwork was sold at auction for a staggering $69 million, making it one of the highest-priced NFT sales to date. This auction marked a turning point for the NFT art movement, bringing attention to the concept of digital art ownership.

Other pioneering NFT artists, such as Pak and Micah Johnson, have also gained popularity for their innovative digital creations. The unique nature of NFTs allows artists to explore interactive, dynamic, and multimedia-rich artworks that push the boundaries of traditional art forms.

Notable NFT Auctions and Record-Breaking Sales

The NFT market has witnessed several high-profile auctions and record-breaking sales that have captured global attention. One of the most notable examples is the sale of Jack Dorsey's first-ever tweet as an NFT. The tweet, "just setting up my Twitter," was sold for $2.9 million, highlighting the allure of owning digital moments and historical artifacts on the blockchain.

Sports collectibles have also seen significant NFT sales. NBA Top Shot, a blockchain-based platform that allows fans to buy, sell, and trade officially licensed NBA collectible highlights, has gained immense popularity. Notable NBA Top Shot moments have been sold for six-figure sums, with basketball enthusiasts eager to own iconic plays from their favorite players.

Another remarkable example is the sale of a virtual property called "Genesis Plaza" within the virtual world of Decentraland. The digital plot of land was sold for over $900,000, showcasing the potential value of virtual real estate NFTs.

Viral NFT Collectibles and Internet Sensations

NFTs have also become a breeding ground for viral internet sensations and memes. One such example is the "Nyan Cat" meme, a pixelated cat with a Pop-Tart body flying through space. The creator, Chris Torres, turned the meme into an NFT and sold it for around $600,000. This highlights the unique ability of NFTs to immortalize internet culture and bring digital memes to life as valuable collectibles.

Similarly, the "Disaster Girl" meme, featuring a young girl smirking in front of a burning house, was also tokenized as an NFT, and sold for a significant sum. These viral NFT collectibles capture moments that resonate with internet users and offer a new way to own and celebrate internet culture.

NFTs and Charitable Initiatives: Using Digital Assets for Social Good

NFTs have also found application in charitable initiatives. Artists, musicians, and celebrities have used NFTs to raise funds for various causes and charities. By auctioning exclusive NFTs, they can engage their fan base while contributing to meaningful social impact.

For example, a series of NFTs representing the works of famous artists, including Picasso and Warhol, were sold at auction, with the proceeds going towards charitable organizations. This demonstrates how NFTs can be a powerful tool for philanthropy and leveraging digital assets for the greater good.

The Role of NFT Platforms and Marketplaces in Driving Adoption

NFT platforms and marketplaces play a crucial role in facilitating the buying, selling, and trading of NFTs. These platforms provide artists, creators, and collectors with a space to showcase and monetize their digital assets. Some of the most popular NFT platforms include OpenSea, Rarible, SuperRare, and NBA Top Shot.

As the NFT market continues to evolve, these platforms are at the forefront of driving adoption and innovation. They provide the infrastructure and user-friendly interfaces for artists and users to participate in the NFT ecosystem.

Challenges and the Future of NFTs

As Non-Fungible Tokens (NFTs) continue to capture the imagination of the digital world, they also face challenges and uncertainties. Let's explore some of the challenges and discuss what the future may hold for NFTs.

Scalability and Environmental Concerns: The Energy Impact of NFTs

One of the major challenges facing NFTs is scalability, especially on certain blockchain networks. As the popularity of NFTs grows, the demand for transactions and smart contracts on the blockchain increases, leading to congestion and higher transaction fees. This can result in slower transaction times and higher costs for users.

Another pressing concern is the environmental impact of NFTs, particularly on energy-intensive blockchain networks like Ethereum. The process of creating and validating NFTs, known as "minting," consumes a significant amount of energy. As more NFTs are minted, the carbon footprint of the blockchain network grows, raising questions about sustainability and ecological responsibility.

NFT Authentication and Copyright Issues: Addressing Ownership Challenges

The uniqueness of NFTs presents new challenges related to authentication and copyright issues. While NFTs are meant to represent ownership of a specific digital asset, there have been instances of unauthorized or counterfeit NFTs being sold in the market.

Ensuring the authenticity of NFTs is essential to maintain trust and confidence in the NFT ecosystem. Blockchain technology can help verify the provenance of NFTs, providing a transparent and immutable record of ownership. However, as the NFT market grows, implementing robust authentication mechanisms will become increasingly crucial.

Copyright infringement is another issue that NFTs face. When artists create NFTs based on copyrighted works without permission, it can lead to legal disputes and ethical concerns. Platforms and marketplaces need to implement policies and mechanisms to protect copyright holders and prevent unauthorized use of copyrighted content.

Speculation, Bubble, or Long-Term Value? Evaluating the NFT Market's Sustainability

The rapid rise of the NFT market has raised questions about whether it is fueled by genuine value or speculative hype. Some critics have likened the NFT craze to a bubble that may burst, causing prices to plummet, and leading to potential losses for investors.

Evaluating the long-term value and sustainability of NFTs is a complex task. While some NFTs hold significant cultural and artistic value, others may be driven primarily by speculation and short-term trading. It will be essential for the NFT market to mature and establish a solid foundation based on genuine utility and intrinsic value.

Regulatory Landscape and Legal Considerations for NFTs

The NFT market operates in a relatively unregulated space, which can create uncertainties and risks for both creators and buyers. Regulatory bodies around the world are closely monitoring the growth of NFTs and exploring how to address legal considerations, such as consumer protection, taxation, and money laundering.

As the NFT market evolves, there may be a need for clearer regulations to protect participants and promote responsible use of

NFTs. Regulatory clarity can provide stability and confidence for artists, investors, and platforms, fostering a healthy and sustainable NFT ecosystem.

NFTs Beyond Hype: Predicting the Future Role of Non-Fungible Tokens in the Digital Economy

Despite the challenges and uncertainties, NFTs have the potential to play a significant role in the future of the digital economy. As technology and blockchain networks evolve, scalability issues may be addressed, making NFT transactions faster and more cost-effective.

Moreover, innovations in blockchain technology, such as layer-two solutions and energy-efficient consensus mechanisms, may help mitigate the environmental impact of NFTs. This would make NFTs a more sustainable and eco-friendly option for digital ownership.

NFTs can also continue to revolutionize various industries beyond art and collectibles. As more creators and companies explore the possibilities of tokenization, NFTs may find applications in fields like education, healthcare, supply chain management, and digital identity.

In conclusion, while Non-Fungible Tokens (NFTs) face challenges related to scalability, environmental impact, authentication, copyright, speculation, and regulation, their future in the digital economy is promising. As technology and market practices evolve, NFTs may find more sustainable and impactful applications. The NFT market's maturation will depend on responsible practices, regulatory clarity, and a collective effort to address the challenges ahead.

What is ApeCoin (APE)

ApeCoin (APE) is a special digital coin designed for the APE ecosystem, a project inspired by popular NFT collections like Bored Ape Yacht Club (BAYC) and Mutant Ape Yacht Club (MAYC). Think of it as the native currency of this creative and decentralized world. The APE token has two main roles. First, it acts as a way for people in the APE community to make decisions. It's like the voting ticket that lets you have a say in how things are run. Second, it's used for all sorts of activities and transactions within the APE ecosystem.

People who hold APE tokens get to vote on important matters in the APE ecosystem. They decide how to use the APE DAO's Ecosystem Fund, which is like a pool of resources for making things happen. A special group called the APE Foundation manages this fund based on what the community wants. The APE Foundation makes sure that the community's decisions are carried out. The initial board members serve for six months, and after that, the APE community votes to pick who will be on the board for the next year.

Here's how APE works:

Currency for the APE World: APE tokens are used as money within the APE ecosystem. You can buy stuff, pay for services, or trade them with others. It's like using dollars or euros, but it's specific to the APE world.

Special Perks: If you have APE tokens, you get access to special things like events, services, games, and cool stuff in the APE world. It's like being a member of an exclusive club.

Encouraging Innovation: APE tokens are also given to creative people who want to build new things in the APE world. If you have a cool idea and use APE tokens, you can get rewards for your work. This encourages more and more exciting projects in the APE ecosystem.

ApeCoin officially entered the scene in March 2022 when it became available for trading on popular crypto platforms, including KuCoin. Although it's relatively new, the concept behind ApeCoin started a few years ago with the creation of NFTs like BAYC and MAYC.

The launch of ApeCoin was a big deal. Most of the APE tokens were put into a fund for the APE ecosystem, giving the community a lot of power. Some tokens were set aside for Yuga Labs (the creators) and for a good cause, the Jane Goodall Legacy Foundation. The rest went to the folks who contributed to the launch and the founders of the BAYC NFT series.

ApeCoin is all about making art, gaming, entertainment, and

events happen in a special APE world. It's not controlled by just one person or company; it's all about the community working together to create something exciting in the world of Web3. So, APE is like the heart that powers the APE world, and the community gets to decide what it does next.

Notes:..

....

....

....

....

....

....

....

....

....

....

....

....

....

....

CHAPTER 10 WHAT IS PROOF OF WORK & PROOF OF STAKE?

Understanding Proof of Work (PoW) and Proof of Stake (PoS)

In the world of cryptocurrencies and blockchain technology, two essential concepts determine how transactions are validated and added to the blockchain: Proof of Work (PoW) and Proof of Stake (PoS). Let's explore these consensus mechanisms in simpler terms.

What are Consensus Mechanisms in Blockchain?

Consensus mechanisms are the rules and protocols that ensure all participants in a decentralized network agree on the state of the blockchain. In other words, they determine how transactions are verified and added to the blockchain's public ledger.

Exploring Proof of Work (PoW) and How It Works

WHAT IS PROOF OF WORK & PROOF OF STAKE?

Proof of Work (PoW) is the original and most widely known consensus mechanism, first introduced by Bitcoin. In PoW, miners compete to solve complex mathematical puzzles using computational power. The first miner to find the correct solution gets to validate and add the next block of transactions to the blockchain.

The process of solving these puzzles is called "mining." Mining requires a lot of computational power and electricity, making it resource-intensive. Once a block is mined, other nodes in the network verify the solution, and if it's correct, the block is added to the blockchain, and the miner is rewarded with newly minted cryptocurrency as an incentive.

Understanding Proof of Stake (PoS) and Its Principles

Proof of Stake (PoS) is a newer consensus mechanism that was developed as an alternative to PoW. In PoS, validators, also known as "stakers," are chosen to create new blocks and validate transactions based on the number of coins they "stake" or hold in the network. In simple terms, the more cryptocurrency a validator holds, the more likely they are to be chosen to validate transactions.

Unlike PoW, PoS does not require miners to compete in solving puzzles, eliminating the need for resource-intensive mining. This makes PoS more energy-efficient and environmentally friendly.

Comparing PoW and PoS: Similarities and Differences

While both PoW and PoS serve the same purpose of achieving consensus, they have some key differences:

- **Energy Consumption:** PoW mining requires a significant amount of electricity due to the computational power needed to solve puzzles. PoS, on the other hand, consumes far less energy since it doesn't involve intensive calculations.

- **Security:** PoW is often praised for its high level of security, as the computational power required to overpower the network is extremely costly. PoS, while secure, relies on the economic incentives of validators, which some argue may be less robust.

- **Decentralization:** PoW is known for its strong decentralization, as anyone with sufficient computing power can participate in mining. PoS, however, may face centralization risks if a few large stakeholders dominate the validation process.

- **Scalability:** Both consensus mechanisms face scalability challenges, but PoS has been proposed as a potential solution due to its lower energy consumption and block generation based on coin holdings.

Comparing Consensus Mechanisms: PoW vs. PoS

In the previous section, we learned about Proof of Work (PoW) and Proof of Stake (PoS) as consensus mechanisms in blockchain networks. Now, let's compare these two approaches to understand their similarities, differences, and implications.

Energy Efficiency: PoW's Resource-Intensive Nature vs. PoS' Eco-Friendly Approach

One of the most significant differences between PoW and PoS

is their energy consumption. PoW mining requires powerful computers to solve complex mathematical puzzles continuously. This process demands a substantial amount of electricity, making it energy-intensive and potentially contributing to environmental concerns.

On the other hand, PoS is designed to be much more energy-efficient. Since validators are chosen based on the amount of cryptocurrency they hold, they don't need to solve resource-intensive puzzles. PoS significantly reduces the environmental impact of consensus, making it a greener alternative to PoW.

Security and Vulnerabilities: Analyzing the Strengths and Weaknesses of PoW and PoS

Both PoW and PoS aim to provide a secure and tamper-resistant network. PoW's security stems from the computational power required to mine blocks. Attackers would need to control a majority of the network's computing power (51% attack) to alter the blockchain, which is prohibitively expensive and practically infeasible for large networks like Bitcoin.

In PoS, the security of the network relies on the assumption that the majority of the cryptocurrency holders are honest. However, PoS may face potential risks of centralization if a few large stakeholders control a significant portion of the coins. This could lead to a "rich get richer" scenario, where the wealthiest participants gain even more influence over the network.

Decentralization and Governance: How PoW and PoS Handle Decision-Making

Decentralization is a crucial aspect of blockchain networks, as it ensures no single entity has complete control over the network. PoW has a reputation for being more decentralized, as anyone with sufficient computational power can participate in mining and contribute to block validation.

In PoS, decentralization depends on the distribution of the cryptocurrency. If a few large stakeholders dominate the validation process, it may lead to a more centralized network. However, various PoS networks employ different mechanisms to encourage decentralization and avoid concentration of power.

Governance is another important consideration in consensus mechanisms. In PoW networks, decisions are generally made through discussions among developers, miners, and community members. In PoS networks, decisions can be influenced by coin holders who can propose and vote on network upgrades or changes.

Scalability and Transaction Speed: Performance Comparison of PoW and PoS

Scalability refers to a blockchain's ability to handle a growing number of transactions efficiently. Both PoW and PoS face scalability challenges, but PoS is often considered more scalable due to its energy-efficient nature and the absence of complex mining processes.

Some PoS networks implement solutions like sharding or layer-two solutions to improve scalability. These techniques partition the blockchain into smaller segments, allowing for parallel processing of transactions and increasing overall network capacity.

In conclusion, both Proof of Work (PoW) and Proof of Stake (PoS) have their strengths and weaknesses. PoW's security and decentralization are well-established, but its energy consumption is a concern. PoS, on the other hand, offers an eco-friendly approach and potential scalability benefits, but its decentralization may depend on the distribution of cryptocurrency holdings.

The choice between PoW and PoS depends on the specific needs and goals of a blockchain network. As technology evolves and new consensus mechanisms are explored, we may witness innovative approaches that combine the best features of both PoW and PoS, contributing to the development of more efficient, secure, and sustainable blockchain networks.

Environmental Impacts and Innovations in Consensus

In the previous sections, we explored the concepts of Proof of Work (PoW) and Proof of Stake (PoS) as consensus mechanisms in blockchain networks. Now, let's delve deeper into the environmental impacts of these mechanisms and explore the innovations aimed at making consensus more sustainable.

The Environmental Concerns of PoW: Energy Consumption

and Carbon Footprint

One of the primary criticisms of PoW is its energy-intensive nature. Mining operations require powerful computer hardware, often in the form of specialized mining rigs, to continuously solve complex mathematical puzzles. As a result, the energy consumption of PoW-based blockchains can be staggering.

Bitcoin, the first and most prominent PoW-based cryptocurrency, is often in the spotlight for its energy usage. According to some estimates, Bitcoin mining consumes as much energy as entire countries. Critics argue that such high energy consumption is unsustainable and has a significant carbon footprint, contributing to climate change.

Green Solutions: Exploring Eco-Friendly Approaches to PoW Mining

Recognizing the environmental concerns associated with PoW, researchers and blockchain enthusiasts have been exploring ways to make mining more eco-friendly.

One approach is to explore renewable energy sources for powering mining operations. Renewable energy, such as solar, wind, or hydroelectric power, provides a greener alternative to fossil fuels. Some mining operations have already transitioned to using renewable energy to power their mining farms, reducing their carbon impact.

Additionally, some blockchain projects are exploring the concept of "proof of useful work." Instead of using computational power solely for mining, this approach leverages the energy expended on solving puzzles to perform useful computations or contribute to scientific research. By doing so, miners' computational power is put to practical use, potentially benefiting fields like medicine, climate research, or data analysis.

PoS as an Environmentally Friendly Alternative: Lowering the Carbon Impact

Proof of Stake offers an eco-friendlier alternative to PoW. By eliminating the need for resource-intensive mining, PoS significantly reduces energy consumption and carbon emissions.

In PoS, validators are selected to create and validate new blocks based on the amount of cryptocurrency they hold and "stake" in the network. Since there is no competitive mining involved, PoS is more energy-efficient, requiring only a fraction of the electricity used in PoW.

As a result, PoS-based blockchains have a considerably lower carbon footprint compared to PoW-based ones. Ethereum, the world's second-largest cryptocurrency, is transitioning from PoW to PoS in its Ethereum 2.0 upgrade to address its energy concerns.

Innovations in Consensus: Hybrid Approaches and Beyond

As the blockchain industry continues to evolve, innovative approaches to consensus mechanisms are being explored. Some projects are experimenting with hybrid consensus models that combine elements of both PoW and PoS.

In hybrid models, PoW may be used as a form of initial distribution or to secure the network during early stages. Then, the blockchain transitions to PoS, where validators take over the block validation process. This approach aims to leverage the strengths of both mechanisms while mitigating their weaknesses.

Beyond PoW and PoS, other consensus mechanisms, such as Delegated Proof of Stake (DPoS), Practical Byzantine Fault Tolerance (PBFT), and Directed Acyclic Graphs (DAGs), are also being researched and implemented. These mechanisms address various challenges, including scalability and energy consumption.

The Future of Consensus Mechanisms: PoW vs. PoS

In the previous sections, we explored Proof of Work (PoW) and Proof of Stake (PoS) as consensus mechanisms in blockchain networks, their environmental impacts, and innovative solutions. Now, let's discuss the future prospects of these mechanisms and their potential roles in the evolving landscape of blockchain technology.

The Role of PoW in Legacy Blockchains and Its Evolution in the Cryptocurrency Space

Proof of Work (PoW) has been the foundation of several prominent cryptocurrencies, including Bitcoin, for over a decade. It has proven to be a robust and secure consensus mechanism, establishing the credibility and immutability of blockchain records.

Despite its success, PoW has faced criticisms due to its energy consumption. However, its position as the original consensus mechanism and its wide adoption in existing blockchains make it a crucial part of the cryptocurrency space.

As the industry advances, some PoW-based projects are exploring ways to become more energy-efficient. They may adopt green mining practices or migrate to alternative consensus mechanisms like Proof of Stake.

PoS' Rise to Prominence: Its Adoption and Potential in Future Blockchain Networks

Proof of Stake (PoS) has gained increasing popularity in recent years due to its energy-efficient and environmentally friendly nature. Ethereum, the second-largest cryptocurrency, is transitioning from PoW to PoS with its Ethereum 2.0 upgrade, aiming to address its energy concerns and improve scalability.

Many new blockchain projects are choosing PoS as their consensus mechanism, attracted by its lower energy consumption and potential for greater decentralization.

In PoS networks, participants are incentivized to act honestly, as their cryptocurrency holdings are at stake. This motivation fosters a cooperative and trustworthy environment, where validators are rewarded for securing the network.

Hybrid Approaches: Exploring Combinations of PoW and

PoS for Optimal Performance

As blockchain technology matures, some projects are exploring hybrid consensus mechanisms that combine PoW and PoS elements. These hybrid approaches aim to leverage the strengths of both mechanisms while mitigating their weaknesses.

For instance, a blockchain network may use PoW for initial distribution or as a security measure during its early stages. Once the network is established, it could transition to PoS, relying on validators to validate transactions.

Hybrid models offer potential benefits, such as enhanced security during the initial launch phase and reduced energy consumption in the later stages.

Shifting Towards Sustainability: The Impact of Consensus Mechanisms on the Blockchain Industry

The quest for sustainability in the blockchain industry is a collective effort. As blockchain technology gains broader adoption, the environmental impact of consensus mechanisms becomes a crucial consideration.

Projects and developers are continuously exploring innovative solutions to address energy consumption concerns and minimize carbon footprints.

Moreover, research and development in the field of blockchain are not limited to PoW and PoS alone. Many other consensus mechanisms, such as Delegated Proof of Stake (DPoS), Practical Byzantine Fault Tolerance (PBFT), and Directed Acyclic Graphs

(DAGs), are gaining attention and adoption in various use cases.

In Conclusion

The future of consensus mechanisms in the blockchain industry is dynamic and multifaceted. PoW and PoS will continue to play significant roles, with PoS gaining prominence due to its energy efficiency.

As technology evolves, hybrid models and other innovative consensus mechanisms will likely emerge, providing a diverse range of options for developers and blockchain networks.

Sustainability and efficiency will remain key focal points as the industry works towards building scalable, secure, and eco-friendly blockchain solutions that can impact various sectors of the global economy.

What is Dash (DASH)

Dash (DASH) is a special type of digital money that's designed to be super-fast, secure, and cheap for making payments online and in person. It's a bit like Bitcoin, but it's made to be more user-friendly and work well for people all around the world. Here are some important things to know about Dash:

Accessible Everywhere: You can use Dash on your computer or on your smartphone. It's designed to be easy to use on all sorts of devices.

Used Worldwide: Just like regular money, you can take out Dash from special ATMs all over the world. This means you can use it like traditional money, which is very convenient.

Accepted by Many: Dash is accepted by more than 150,000 businesses and services all around the world. This means you can use it to pay for things both online and in physical stores.

Fast Transactions: One of Dash's special features is its super-fast transaction speed. It takes only one second to process a payment. This makes it useful for everyday stuff.

DASH Coin: DASH is the special cryptocurrency of the Dash system. You can use it to send and receive payments and to buy things online and in stores. DASH coins are created when people use the Dash system. They are given as rewards to the people who help make the system work, like miners and Master nodes.

Now, let's look at how Dash Coin works:

1. Miners and Master nodes: Dash works a lot like Bitcoin, using something called Proof of Work. It has miners who check and approve transactions, and it also has something called Master nodes that do special jobs.

2. Instant Payments: Dash is known for its fast transactions, thanks to Masternodes. They help make sure your payments are super quick.

3. Privacy: Dash also takes privacy seriously. It has a feature called CoinJoin that makes your transactions more private.

4. Security: Dash has a feature called ChainLocks to keep your money safe from possible attacks.

5. Community Power: Users of Dash get to have a say in how the system works. They use a part of the rewards from the system to make decisions and improve Dash.

6. Next-Gen Payment System: Dash is working on something called Dash Evolution. It's like the next big thing in making payments with cryptocurrency. It aims to be as easy to use as PayPal, but with all the benefits of cryptocurrency.

7. Being a Masternode: To be a Masternode, you need to own 1,000 DASH coins as a sort of promise. This helps make the Dash system more secure.

8. Earning Rewards: If you become a Masternode, you get rewarded with 45% of the system's rewards. It's like a thank-you for helping to keep Dash running smoothly.

Now, let's go back in time a bit to see how Dash started:

- Dash was created by Evan Duffield and a group of visionaries who wanted to make a cryptocurrency that's easy to use and great for everyday transactions.

- In January 2014, they launched Dash.

- Over the years, they added important features like PrivateSend for privacy, Instant Send for speedy transactions, and a treasury system that helps improve and grow the Dash system.

- A big moment came in 2017 when Dash made its transaction fees much lower, making it even more affordable to use.

- And in 2019, they rebranded Dash Evolution as Dash Platform, which lets developers create cool apps on the Dash system.

So, Dash is all about making it easy for everyone to use cryptocurrency for everyday payments, and it keeps getting better and more exciting!

COIN LIST TO WATCH

....

....

....

....

....

....

....

....

....

....

....

....

....

What is Monero (XMR)

Monero (XMR) is a cryptocurrency that takes privacy and anonymity very seriously. It's all about giving people the ability to make transactions without anyone snooping on them. It's one of the most popular privacy-focused cryptocurrencies out there. Here's how it works:

Protecting Your Privacy: Monero was made to allow people to make transactions without worrying about someone tracking them. Most other cryptocurrencies show lots of information about who is sending money to whom and how much. Monero doesn't. It uses three important technologies to hide this information:

- **Stealth Addresses:** These make it hard to figure out who is receiving the money.

- **Ring Signatures:** These mix up the transactions, so you can't tell who is sending money to whom.

- **RingCT**: This hides the amount of XMR being sent in a transaction.

Staying Anonymous Online: All Monero transactions happen using special networks like Tor/I2P. These networks are designed to keep things anonymous. So when you use Monero, it's like being in a secret club where no one knows who you are.

Keeping Money Clean: XMR is what's called "fungible." That means that one XMR coin is just like any other XMR coin. There's no way to tell if a coin has been used for something good or something bad in the past. This is really important for businesses and people who want to use clean money.

Quick and Cheap: Monero transactions are fast and don't cost much. It's a great way to send money, and it's way cheaper than traditional banking.

Monero works with a system called Proof of Work to keep the network secure and make sure all the transactions are correct. Miners are like the police of the network. They use special equipment to check transactions and add them to the blockchain. For their work, they get rewards in the form of XMR.

So, what can you do with XMR?

1. Make Digital Payments: You can use XMR to pay for things online and in person. It's like using digital cash that's super fast and private.

2. Invest and Trade: XMR is one of the oldest and most well-known cryptocurrencies. It's a good choice for people who want to invest and trade in the crypto world. But remember to do your research and keep an eye on XMR's price and market trends.

3. Earn Passive Income: If you have some XMR, you can lend it on platforms like KuCoin and earn extra money. It's a way to grow your XMR without doing much work.

4. Become a Miner: If you want to help the Monero network and make some XMR in the process, you can become a miner. Miners check transactions and add them to the blockchain, and they get rewards for their hard work.

WHAT IS PROOF OF WORK & PROOF OF STAKE?

Monero's main goal is to keep your transactions private and secure, and it's a great choice if you want to use cryptocurrency in a way that's safe and discreet.

CHAPTER 11 WHAT ARE SMART CONTRACTS?

Unveiling the Concept of Smart Contracts

Imagine if contracts could execute themselves without relying on a middleman or a court of law. That's the power of smart contracts, a fascinating concept that brings together technology and legal agreements in the world of blockchain. In this section, we'll dive into the world of smart contracts, exploring what they are and how they work.

Introducing Smart Contracts: Beyond Traditional Contracts

Traditionally, contracts are formal agreements that outline the terms and conditions between parties. These can range from rental agreements and employment contracts to buying a house. But here's the twist: smart contracts take these traditional agreements and digitize them using code and blockchain technology.

The Role of Code in Self-Executing Agreements

At the heart of a smart contract is code, a set of instructions that define the terms of the agreement. This code operates on the "if-then" principle. If certain conditions are met, then the contract executes automatically. For instance, consider a rental agreement: if the tenant pays the rent on time, then the smart contract releases the digital key to access the rented property.

How Smart Contracts Utilize Blockchain Technology

Smart contracts are built on blockchain platforms like Ethereum. Blockchain is a digital ledger that records transactions in a secure and transparent manner. The decentralized nature of blockchain ensures that no single entity has control over the contract's execution, enhancing security and trust.

The blockchain provides the foundation for smart contracts to operate. When the conditions defined in the smart contract are met, the contract's execution is recorded on the blockchain. This creates an immutable record of the agreement, ensuring transparency and reducing the chances of disputes.

In simple terms, smart contracts merge the rules of a traditional contract with the automation capabilities of code and the security of blockchain.

Benefits of Smart Contracts

Smart contracts offer several benefits:

• **Trust:** Smart contracts execute automatically when conditions are met, reducing the need for intermediaries, and enhancing trust between parties.

• **Transparency:** Transactions and contract executions are recorded on the blockchain, providing an open and transparent record for all parties to see.

• **Efficiency:** Automation eliminates the need for manual execution and paperwork, saving time and resources.

• **Security:** Blockchain's encryption and decentralization make smart contracts secure and tamper-resistant.

Understanding Self-Executing Contracts on the Blockchain

In the previous section, we introduced the concept of smart contracts and their potential to revolutionize traditional agreements. Now, let's delve deeper into how smart contracts actually work, how they achieve self-execution and the role of decentralization in this process.

From Code to Execution: How Smart Contracts Work

Think of a smart contract as a digital vending machine. When you put in the required amount and press a button (meet the conditions), the machine automatically dispenses the chosen item (executes the contract). Similarly, smart contracts use code to define conditions and actions, ensuring that if those conditions are met, the contract automatically carries out the specified tasks.

For instance, imagine you're buying concert tickets using a smart contract. The code could be set up so that if you send the required amount of cryptocurrency before a certain date, the contract automatically sends you a digital ticket that grants access to the concert.

Automation and Trust in Smart Contracts

Smart contracts rely on automation to function seamlessly. This automation reduces the need for intermediaries such as lawyers or brokers to oversee and enforce contracts. Because the contract's execution is programmed and transparent, it eliminates the potential for misunderstandings or disputes that might arise from the interpretation of traditional contracts.

This automation also enhances trust between parties. You don't have to worry about the other party not fulfilling their part of the deal, because the smart contract ensures that everyone adheres to the agreed-upon terms.

Exploring the Role of Decentralization in Smart Contract Execution

One of the key features of smart contracts is decentralization. Unlike traditional contracts that rely on a central authority (like a court) to enforce them, smart contracts operate on decentralized blockchain networks.

Decentralization means that no single entity has complete control over the execution of the contract. Instead, the execution is verified and validated by multiple participants in the network. This reduces the risk of fraud or manipulation, as altering a smart contract's execution would require consensus from the majority of participants.

Because smart contracts are stored on a blockchain, they are tamper-resistant and transparent. Once a contract's conditions are met and it's executed, the result is recorded on the blockchain, creating an immutable and auditable record.

Real-World Examples

Smart contracts have applications in various industries. For instance:

- **Supply Chain Management:** Smart contracts can track the movement of goods, automatically triggering actions like releasing payments when specific milestones are met.

- **Insurance:** Claims processing can be automated through smart contracts, reducing paperwork, and speeding up the settlement process.

- **Real Estate:** Property transfers can be automated, eliminating the need for intermediaries like real estate agents.

Real-Life Applications of Smart Contracts

In the previous sections, we explored how smart contracts work and their self-executing nature. Now, let's take a closer look at the real-life applications of smart contracts across different industries, showcasing how these digital agreements are making processes more efficient and reliable.

Transforming Industries: How Smart Contracts Impact Various Sectors

Smart contracts are like digital helpers that automate tasks based on predefined rules. Their applications are vast and span across industries:

- **Finance and Banking:** Smart contracts are revolutionizing how financial transactions are conducted. For instance, they can automate the process of transferring ownership of assets, like real estate or stocks, without the need for intermediaries. This reduces delays and costs associated with traditional processes.

- **Supply Chain Management:** In supply chains, smart contracts can monitor the movement of goods. Imagine a shipment of perishable goods that needs to be maintained at a specific temperature. A smart contract could automatically trigger alerts or actions if the temperature deviates, ensuring the goods remain in optimal condition.

- **Healthcare:** Smart contracts can help manage patient data securely. A patient's medical records could be stored in a blockchain, and access could be granted to authorized parties only when specific conditions are met, ensuring patient privacy and data accuracy.

- **Insurance:** Claims processing can be expedited with smart contracts. When certain conditions, such as a flight delay, are met, the contract could automatically release compensation to the policyholder without the need for manual claims processing.

Smart Contracts in Finance: Streamlining Transactions and Agreements

The financial sector is experiencing a significant impact from smart contracts. Traditional financial transactions often involve multiple intermediaries, paperwork, and time delays. Smart contracts automate these processes, reducing the need for intermediaries and streamlining transactions.

- **Decentralized Finance (DeFi):** DeFi is an emerging trend that leverages smart contracts to recreate traditional financial services in a decentralized manner. Through DeFi platforms, individuals can lend, borrow, trade, and earn interest on their crypto assets without relying on traditional banks or financial institutions.

- **Mortgages and Loans:** Smart contracts can automate the approval and management of loans and mortgages. They can ensure that borrowers meet specific conditions (like credit scores) before funds are disbursed, and automatically deduct repayments based on predefined schedules.

Supply Chain Management and Transparency with Smart Contracts

Supply chain management involves numerous parties, from manufacturers to distributors. Smart contracts can improve transparency and efficiency across the supply chain:

- **Verification and Tracking:** Smart contracts can ensure the authenticity of products by recording their journey from production to delivery. This helps combat counterfeiting and provides consumers with confidence in the origin and quality of products.

- **Automated Payments:** When goods reach specific checkpoints in the supply chain, smart contracts can trigger automatic payments. For instance, a supplier might receive payment as soon as their products arrive at the warehouse.

- **Reducing Disputes:** Smart contracts provide a tamper-resistant record of all transactions in the supply chain. This can help resolve disputes quickly by providing an auditable history of events.

Challenges and Future Directions of Smart Contracts

In the previous sections, we explored the real-world applications of smart contracts and how they are transforming various industries. Now, let's delve into some of the challenges that smart contracts face and the exciting possibilities that lie ahead.

Addressing Security Concerns in Smart Contract Execution

While smart contracts offer many benefits, they are not immune to challenges. One significant concern is security. Smart contracts are executed based on the code written, and any vulnerabilities in the code can be exploited by malicious actors. Such vulnerabilities can lead to unintended outcomes or even theft of funds.

To address this, extensive code auditing, testing, and peer review are essential before deploying a smart contract.

Additionally, developers are exploring innovative techniques to enhance the security of smart contracts and minimize the risks associated with potential vulnerabilities.

The Evolution of Smart Contract Standards and Interoperability

Another challenge in the world of smart contracts is the lack of standardized practices and protocols. Different blockchain platforms may have varying smart contract languages and architectures. This lack of uniformity can hinder cross-platform compatibility and interoperability.

Efforts are being made to establish common standards for smart contracts that work across different blockchains. These standards would ensure that smart contracts can seamlessly interact with each other, promoting interoperability and expanding their potential applications.

Smart Contracts Beyond Blockchain: Integrating with IoT and AI Technologies

The future of smart contracts is not limited to just blockchains. They have the potential to integrate with other cutting-edge technologies:

- **Internet of Things (IoT):** Smart contracts can automate interactions between IoT devices. For example, if the temperature in a warehouse exceeds a certain limit, a smart contract could automatically trigger actions like adjusting the thermostat or alerting the manager.

- **Artificial Intelligence (AI):** AI-powered smart contracts could dynamically adjust contract terms based on real-time data. For instance, in an insurance contract, the terms and premium could be adjusted based on the policyholder's driving behavior captured by AI-driven sensors in their vehicle.

- **Blockchain's Social Impact:** Smart contracts are also contributing to social impact initiatives. They can help provide financial services to the unbanked population, facilitate transparent charitable donations, and enable secure identity management for refugees and marginalized communities.

- Decentralization, a core feature of smart contracts, empowers individuals by allowing them to have direct control over their assets and data. This can lead to a more inclusive and equitable financial landscape.

The Path Forward: Continuous Innovation

As the technology landscape evolves, smart contracts will likely continue to evolve as well. Developers are working on solutions to make smart contract development more user-friendly, enabling wider adoption. Research into enhancing smart contract privacy and scalability is ongoing to address their limitations in these areas.

In conclusion, while smart contracts offer immense potential, they also face challenges related to security, standardization, and compatibility. However, the ongoing efforts to address these challenges and the integration with other emerging technologies make the future of smart contracts exciting and promising.

Will Shiba Inu Coin Achieve $1

In the ever-changing environment of cryptocurrency markets, a distinct category known as "meme coins" has arisen, drawing both attention and investment.

Among these, Shiba Inu (SHIB) has garnered significant interest from both industry experts and cryptocurrency fans.

The quick growth of SHIB has prompted an urgent inquiry that has reverberated across financial forums and professional analyses: Will Shiba Inu hit the momentous milestone of $1 in the near future?

In this in-depth examination, we will investigate all possible circumstances, opportunities, and obstacles with Shiba Inu in order to answer this burning question.

Overview of the Shiba Inu

Shiba Inu is a decentralized meme token named after the Japanese dog breed that was launched in August 2020. It is marketed as the "Doge Killer," with the goal of providing a new perspective in the world of cryptocurrencies.

Shiba Inu Development Story

Shiba Inu was created and listed on minor exchanges in August

2020, amid a rising trend in meme coins. SHIB was initially a niche and underground token, accessible exclusively through tiny exchanges and decentralized trade platforms.

SHIB was created with the goal of establishing a community-driven cryptocurrency rather than concentrating authority inside a single organisation.

While the coin's price remained low and trading volume was low, its innovative concept and dedicated community lay the framework for future growth.

Significant Price Increases and Major Exchange Listings - 2021 was a watershed year for Shiba Inu, with dramatic price increase and popular acceptance.

The coin had remarkable price increases, particularly during the spring months. This spike was spurred by a combination of celebrity endorsements, social media chatter, and the broader cryptocurrency bull market. SHIB has been listed on major exchanges such as Binance, Coinbase, and Kraken, increasing its accessibility and legitimacy.

Shiba Inu has established itself as a key player in the crypto ecosystem by the end of 2021, drawing a diversified investment base and earning a multi-billion dollar market valuation.

Community Growth and Market Penetration - As the year 2022 approached, Shiba Inu's attention changed to sustainability, utility, and long-term growth. The development team pioneered new use cases, such as ShibaSwap, an exchange platform, and worked with multiple shops to accept SHIB as payment.

These initiatives intended to elevate SHIB from a joke coin to a viable cryptocurrency with real-world applications. The community grew rapidly as well as active participation in governance, development, and marketing operations.

Furthermore, the team's charitable and global outreach initiatives aided in expanding market penetration, retaining momentum, and establishing Shiba Inu as more than just a passing fad.

Shiba Inu Current Stats

Price (as of writing): $0.000007091

Market Cap: $4.17 Billion

Circulating Supply: 589.34T SHIB

Will the Shiba Inu ever reach $1?

Shiba Inu will not be able to achieve $1 with the present tokenomics. Consider this: to achieve $1, Shiba Inu would have to increase by more than 12,800,000% from where it is currently. That is no easy task!

There are a few factors that could spark a bullish run for this parody coin. But what about attaining that $1 target? That's a very different story.

Here's something to think about: It gets more difficult for something to continue growing at the same rate as it grows larger. It's like the snowball effect, but in reverse.

When you're starting off, minor gains in adoption or other

enhancements can make a big difference, but as you develop, the same changes don't have the same impact.

That explains why Shiba Inu was able to achieve such astounding results.

throughout 2021 trade. It began as a small puppy and grew into a large dog!

But it's a different ballgame now. Shiba Inu's initial price has already climbed more than predicted. So, while the rise to $1 may appear less in percentage points when compared to what it's already done, pulling it off is a feat.

How Do Shiba Inu and Dogecoin Compare?

Shiba Inu is sometimes compared to Dogecoin, as both began as meme coins. While they have some thematic overlap, they differ in terms of technology, community goals, use cases, and market tactics. A thorough comparison would necessitate an examination of specific factors such as tokenomics, development roadmaps, and community engagement.

YOUR FUTURE INVESTMENT SELF-BRAINSTROMING

....

....

....

....

....

CHAPTER 12 WHAT IS STABLECOIN?

Understanding Stablecoins and Their Price Stability

Cryptocurrencies have gained attention for their potential to revolutionize finance, but their wild price swings can sometimes make them risky for everyday use. This is where stablecoins come into play, offering a solution that combines the benefits of cryptocurrencies with the stability of traditional currencies. In this section, we'll dive into what stablecoins are and how they maintain their price stability.

Introducing Stablecoins: Cryptocurrencies with a Predictable Value

Stablecoins are a special category of cryptocurrencies designed to have a steady value, often pegged to a stable asset like a traditional currency (e.g., US Dollar) or a commodity (e.g., gold).

While traditional cryptocurrencies like Bitcoin and Ethereum can experience significant price fluctuations within a short period, stablecoins aim to provide a more predictable value.

How Stablecoins Maintain Price Stability in the Volatile Crypto Market

The key to stablecoins' price stability lies in their underlying mechanism. Let's look at a couple of common types:

Fiat-Collateralized Stablecoins: These stablecoins are backed by reserves of traditional currencies or other assets. For example, for every stablecoin issued, there might be a corresponding US Dollar held in a bank account. This ensures that the value of the stablecoin is linked to a tangible asset, maintaining its stability.

Crypto-Collateralized Stablecoins: Instead of traditional currency, these stablecoins are backed by other cryptocurrencies. Smart contracts are used to ensure that the value of the collateral exceeds the value of the stablecoins issued. If the value of the stablecoin drops, the collateral is automatically liquidated to stabilize the price.

Algorithmic Stablecoins: These stablecoins use algorithms and smart contracts to control their supply and demand, maintaining a stable value. For instance, if the price of the stablecoin rises, the algorithm might issue more coins to bring the price down.

Stablecoins offers a bridge between the world of cryptocurrencies and traditional finance. They provide a way to transact and store value using blockchain technology without being exposed to the extreme volatility associated with other cryptocurrencies.

Benefits and Use Cases of Stablecoins

Stablecoins offer several benefits:

Payment and Remittances: Stablecoins can be used for everyday transactions, similar to traditional currencies. They can also facilitate cross-border remittances, allowing people to send money quickly and with lower fees.

Decentralized Finance (DeFi): Stablecoins are a cornerstone of the DeFi ecosystem. They provide a stable unit of account within DeFi platforms where users can lend, borrow, and trade without worrying about price volatility.

Hedging: Traders and investors can use stablecoins to hedge against the price fluctuations of other cryptocurrencies. If they expect a market downturn, they can convert their assets into stablecoins to preserve value.

Reducing Volatility: Stablecoins can act as a stable store of value during times of market turbulence, offering a safe haven for those looking to protect their wealth.

The Role of Stablecoins in the Crypto Ecosystem

In the previous section, we explored the concept of stablecoins and how they maintain price stability. Now, let's delve into the crucial role that stablecoins play in the broader cryptocurrency ecosystem and their impact on various aspects of finance and technology.

The Importance of Stability in the World of Cryptocurrencies

Cryptocurrencies, while revolutionary, have faced criticism due to their extreme price volatility. Imagine buying something with a cryptocurrency, only to find that its value has significantly changed the next day. This unpredictability can be a barrier to their widespread adoption for everyday transactions.

Stablecoins step in to address this issue by providing a reliable and stable unit of account within the crypto ecosystem. They bridge the gap between the benefits of blockchain technology and the stability of traditional currencies.

Use Cases and Benefits of Stablecoins in Decentralized Finance (DeFi)

One of the most exciting areas where stablecoins shine is in the world of Decentralized Finance (DeFi). DeFi aims to recreate traditional financial services using blockchain technology, and stablecoins are central to its operation.

- **Lending and Borrowing:** DeFi platforms allow users to lend their crypto assets and earn interest, or borrow against their assets without the need for a traditional bank. Stablecoins are a natural fit here. Lenders can earn interest on their stablecoins, and borrowers can access loans without worrying about the volatility of other cryptocurrencies.

- **Decentralized Exchanges**: Stablecoins serve as a reliable trading pair on decentralized exchanges, enabling traders to move in and out of the crypto market without exposing themselves to the risk of price fluctuations.

Stablecoins in Payment Systems and Remittances

Stablecoins also play a vital role in simplifying cross-border transactions. Traditional international money transfers can be slow and expensive. By using stablecoins, individuals can send money across borders in a matter of minutes with minimal fees.

Imagine someone working abroad who wants to send money back home to their family. Using stablecoins, they can bypass the traditional banking system and transfer funds directly and quickly.

Cryptocurrency Adoption and Mainstream Use

Stablecoins have the potential to increase the adoption of cryptocurrencies among the masses. The stable value of these coins makes them more suitable for everyday transactions like buying goods, paying for services, or even receiving a salary.

As people become more familiar with using stablecoins, they might also be more inclined to explore other aspects of the crypto world. This could lead to increased interest in cryptocurrencies with higher volatility, like Bitcoin and Ethereum.

Stablecoins as a Gateway to Blockchain Technology

For individuals who are new to cryptocurrencies, stablecoins can serve as an entry point into the world of blockchain technology. Their stability and ease of use make them a less intimidating introduction to crypto space.

In conclusion, stablecoins are a linchpin in the cryptocurrency ecosystem. By providing price stability, they enable a wide range of applications, from DeFi and remittances to mainstream adoption. As technology continues to evolve, stablecoins have the potential to reshape how we transact and interact with financial systems.

Innovations and Challenges in the Stablecoin Landscape

Having explored the significance of stablecoins and their role in the cryptocurrency ecosystem, let's delve into the diverse types of stablecoins, their advantages, and the challenges they face as they continue to evolve.

Exploring Different Types of Stablecoins

Stablecoins come in various flavors, each with its own unique mechanism to maintain price stability:

- **Fiat-Collateralized Stablecoins:** These stablecoins are directly backed by reserves of traditional currencies, such as the US Dollar. Each stablecoin issued corresponds to an equivalent amount of the underlying fiat currency held in a reserve. Tether (USDT) and USD Coin (USDC) are examples of fiat-collateralized stablecoins.

- **Crypto-Collateralized Stablecoins:** These stablecoins are backed by other cryptocurrencies, often in a higher value than the stablecoin itself. Smart contracts ensure that the collateral value exceeds the stablecoin's value. For example, if you're issuing stablecoins worth $100, you might need to lock up $150 worth of Ethereum as collateral.

- **Algorithmic Stablecoins:** Algorithmic stablecoins, like DAI, don't rely on direct collateral but rather use algorithms and smart contracts to maintain stability. If the price of the stablecoin goes above its peg, the algorithm might issue new stablecoins to decrease the price.

Stablecoins' Regulatory and Security Challenges

Despite their potential, stablecoins face challenges on both regulatory and security fronts:

Regulatory Scrutiny: Stablecoins that are pegged to traditional currencies have caught the attention of regulatory bodies around the world. Authorities are concerned about their potential impact on financial stability and are evaluating how to regulate them effectively.

Centralization Concerns: Some stablecoins have faced criticism for being overly centralized, especially those with single entities controlling the reserves. This goes against the decentralized ethos of cryptocurrencies.

Smart Contract Vulnerabilities: Just like other cryptocurrencies, stablecoins can face smart contract vulnerabilities. Flaws in the code or vulnerabilities in the platform they're built on can lead to unintended consequences.

Future Innovations in Stablecoins

The stablecoin landscape is continually evolving with new innovations to address these challenges:

- **Decentralized Collateral:** Some projects are working on stablecoins with decentralized collateral to ensure greater security and decentralization.

- **Enhanced Regulation:** Stablecoin projects are collaborating with regulators to ensure compliance and address concerns, which could lead to increased acceptance.

- **Interoperability:** Projects are exploring ways to improve the interoperability between different stablecoins and blockchain platforms, allowing for seamless conversions.

In Conclusion

Stablecoins have emerged as a vital bridge between the traditional financial world and the innovative realm of cryptocurrencies. Their diverse types and mechanisms cater to various needs within the ecosystem. As the stablecoin landscape continues to evolve, addressing regulatory concerns and enhancing security will be crucial for their sustained growth and mainstream adoption.

The Fall of Terra: A Timeline of UST and LUNA's Meteoric Rise and Crash

A detailed chronology of Terra's path from its humble beginnings as a payment's app in South Korea to a $60 billion crypto ecosystem to one of cryptocurrency's biggest flops.

The Terra network and its leader, Do Kwon, soared to the top of the cryptocurrency market thanks to big-name investors, only to collapse in a matter of days in May 2022.

The price of the then-$18-billion algorithmic stablecoin terraUSD (UST), which is designed to keep a $1 peg, began to sway on May 7 and plummeted to 35 cents on May 9. Its partner token, LUNA, which was supposed to stabilize the price of UST, dropped from $80 to a few cents by May 12. What follows is a detailed timeline of the Terra blockchain's history, including Do Kwon's vision to create a price-stable crypto payment system to compete with the largest e-commerce platforms, Terra becoming one of the most popular red-hot crypto projects, Do Kwon's growing antics on social media, and how it all came crashing down in the end, wiping out the life savings of desperate everyday investors.

2018

- Do Kwon and Daniel Shin launch the Terra network in

January 2018, with ambitions to produce Chai, an e-commerce payments application, as well as a price-stable cryptocurrency versus major fiat currencies to support transactions. It is backed by the Terra Alliance, a group of 15 major Asian e-commerce enterprises.

- April 20: Cyrus Younessi, head of risk at MakerDAO and a former Scaler research analyst, explains Scaler why he believes Terra/LUNA will fail, predicting a scenario that will play out in mid-2022.

- Terraform Labs, the company behind the Terra blockchain, is founded in Singapore on April 23.

2019

- On January 30, LUNA is sold to investors through an initial coin offering. During a seed round, Terraform Labs charged 18 cents per token and 80 cents per token during a private sale.

- Do Kwon and many co-authors released the Terra Money white paper in April.

2020

- The first LUNA staking product is launched on February 24 by a South Korean crypto exchange.

- On July 6, Terra's head of research, Nicholas Platt, announces the Anchor protocol, a platform based on Terra that allows investors to earn a high rate on their deposits while simultaneously borrowing against their crypto assets.

- The Terra blockchain's stablecoin, UST, is publicly revealed on September 21st, with intentions to deploy on Ethereum and Solana.

- Mirror, Terra's synthetic stock system, becomes live on December 3.

2021

- The Securities and Exchange Commision subpoenas Terraform Labs founder Do Kwon on September 21st, citing worries that Mirror may violate federal securities legislation.

- Do Kwon rules out a George Soros-style attack on UST/LUNA, which may drive it into a death spiral, on November 28. Some would later argue, in mid-2022, that this is the type of event that caused Terra's demise.

- LUNA's price nearly doubled to new highs above $90 on December 22nd and is up 58% this month.

Early 2022

- Do Kwon announces the formation of Luna Foundation Guard, an organization "mandated to build reserves supporting the $UST peg amid volatile market conditions" as well as "allocate resources supporting the growth and development of the Terra ecosystem" through grants on January 19.

- Jump Crypto and Three Arrows Capital are the principal investors in the $1 billion LUNA token sale by Singapore-based Luna Foundation Guard (LFG) to buy bitcoin for UST's reserve system.

• Do Kwon announces the formation of Luna Foundation Guard, an organization "mandated to build reserves supporting the $UST peg amid volatile market conditions" as well as "allocate resources supporting the growth and development of the Terra ecosystem" through grants on January 19.

• Jump Crypto and Three Arrows Capital are the principal investors in the $1 billion LUNA token sale by Singapore-based Luna Foundation Guard (LFG) to buy bitcoin for UST's reserve system.

March 2022

• March 13: Crypto trader Algod, who compares UST/LUNA to a Ponzi scheme, wagers $1 million against Do Kwon that LUNA will be worth less than $88 by March of next year. Another cryptocurrency trader, GiganticRebirth, is betting $10 million against Kwon that LUNA will be worth less than $88 by next year.

• March 23: Do Kwon tweets "By my hand, DAI will die" as he launches serious measures to starve decentralised stablecoin DAI of liquidity on Curve.

• Jump Trading, one of the investors behind LFG, suggests a mechanism for deploying bitcoin (BTC) reserves to prop up the price of UST in a crisis on March 23.

• March 25: Rumours circulate that LFG purchased $125 million (2,840 BTC) in bitcoin.

- March 28: The Luna Foundation Guard's bitcoin wallet address has purchased over 27,000 BTC worth about $1.3 billion in the last six days.

- Terra's LUNA coins have risen 10% in the last 24 hours to new all-time highs of more than $106.

- "Grandpa, what was the world like when $LUNA was less than three digits?" tweets Kyle Davies, co-founder of influential trading firm Three Arrows Capital, on March 29.

- This week, LFG purchased 5,773 BTC for $272 million.

April 2022

- According to crypto analysis firm Messari, the price of the LUNA coin reaches an all-time high of $119.2 on April 5.

- LFG purchases 5,040 BTC on April 6, bringing its total holdings to 35,768 BTC, valued at $1.6 billion at the time.

- LFG purchases $100 million in AVAX with UST stablecoins on April 7.

- April 11: Over the weekend, LFG adds $173 million in bitcoin to its wallet through a series of purchases. Its wallet now contains 39,897.98 bitcoin.

- Terraform Labs grants LFG 10 million LUNA tokens valued $820 million on April 14.

- April 19, 2022: LUNA beats the overall crypto market with a 17% increase in a single day, sending values above $90. UST is now the third most valuable stablecoin.

- April 27: The circulating supply of LUNA reaches an all-time low of 346 million tokens as LUNA tokens are burned to meet surging UST demand.

May 2022

- Curve Whale Watching, a bot that tracks and tweets enormous amounts of swaps, shows an 85 million UST swap for 84.5 million USDC on May 7.

- May 7: After a series of huge dumps of UST on Terra's lending protocol Anchor and stablecoin exchange protocol Curve, UST fell to a low of $0.985 on Saturday.

- May 8: LFG agrees to lending $750 million in BTC to market makers to protect the UST peg, and another $750 million in UST will be used to purchase back BTC after volatility has subsided.

- Do Kwon chuckles his way out of UST's DE pegging peril on May 8.

- May 9: Anchor protocol deposits fall below $9 billion from $14 billion as UST fails to return to $1. The protocol's token, ANC, dropped 35% during the day.

- May 9: UST loses its one-dollar peg for the second time, falling as low as 35 cents.

- Do Kwon tweets on May 9th, "Deploying more capital - steady lads."

- May 10: Claims that UST's depreciation is the result of a Soros-style campaign arise.

- May 11: Despite Tuesday's dip, 58% of traders place futures bets on higher LUNA prices, resulting in $63 million in liquidations.

- May 11: LUNA reaches levels last seen in August 2021. Anchor, Terra's largest decentralized finance (DeFi) protocol, has lost $11 billion in value in two days.

- Do Kwon has been unmasked as one of the pseudonymous co-founders of the failed algorithmic stablecoin Basis Cash, according to CoinDesk.

- May 12: The LUNA price drops 96% in a single day, reaching less than 10 cents.

- May 12: The Terra blockchain is officially paused for the first time, at block height 7603700, as the price of LUNA plummets precipitously, jeopardising the network's security.

- May 12: The Terra blockchain is suspended for the second time at block 7607789, although activity resumes after around nine hours.

- The Okx and Binance exchanges stop selling Terra tokens on May 13th, after UST loses its dollar peg and LUNA drops by more than 99%. Binance later resumes LUNA trading.

- Do Kwon presents a "Revival Plan" on May 13 that would see network ownership handed to UST and LUNA holders via 1 billion new tokens.

- Elliptic, a data analytics startup, followed LFG's $3.5 billion BTC reserve to major exchanges Gemini and Binance on May 14.

- May 16: LFG acknowledges that during the attempt to save UST's peg, it drained its BTC reserves from about 80,000 bitcoins to 313 bitcoins.

- Do Kwon offers a Terra fork without UST, naming the present chain "Terra Classic."

- May 19: Hashed, a notable Terra-backer venture firm based in Seoul, South Korea, looks to have lost more than $3.5 billion because of the Terra debacle.

- May 20: Terra's decentralized banking apps have lost $28 billion in value as investors have mainly abandoned the Terra ecosystem.

- May 24: South Korean officials are allegedly aiming to more carefully scrutinise cryptocurrency exchanges, after an estimated 280,000 citizens were affected by the sudden drop in UST and LUNA.

- May 25: Terra validators vote to endorse Do Kwon's idea to establish a new blockchain dubbed "Terra 2.0" that will not include a stablecoin. Previous LUNA and UST holders will get Luna (LUNA), the new blockchain's native coin, based on their holdings. The previous Terra blockchain is still operational, and its token has been renamed Luna Classic (LUNC).

- May 27: Nansen, a blockchain data analytics business, publishes its analysis on what transpired during UST's death spiral. The report debunks the idea that the depeg was triggered by a single attacker.

- Terra 2.0 will be released on May 28th, followed by the LUNA airdrop.

CHAPTER 13 WHAT IS TOKEN?

Exploring the Concept of Tokens

Tokens are like the building blocks of the blockchain world, adding extra layers of functionality beyond just cryptocurrencies. In this section, we'll dive into what tokens are, how they differ from cryptocurrencies and altcoins, and how they play a crucial role in the broader blockchain ecosystem.

Demystifying Tokens: Beyond Cryptocurrencies and Altcoins

While tokens and cryptocurrencies are closely related, they aren't quite the same thing. Cryptocurrencies like Bitcoin and Ethereum are digital forms of money that operate on their own blockchains. Tokens, on the other hand, are created and managed on existing blockchains, often using the technology of a cryptocurrency like Ethereum.

Think of cryptocurrencies as the main characters in a story, and tokens as the tools and objects that enhance the story. Tokens can represent almost anything of value—property, real-world assets, memberships, voting rights, and more. They bring flexibility and a wider range of use cases to the blockchain ecosystem.

Understanding How Tokens Add Functionality to the Blockchain Ecosystem

Tokens are the way blockchain projects can represent ownership or access rights within their platforms. They're like digital assets that can be owned, traded, or used to access certain features. For instance:

- In a gaming platform, tokens can represent in-game items, characters, or even ownership in virtual properties.

- Social media platforms might issue tokens that reward users for contributing content or engagement, creating an incentive for participation.

- Companies can issue tokens as part of an Initial Coin Offering (ICO) to raise funds for a project, offering backers a stake in the project's success.

Tokens enhance the blockchain experience by introducing a layer of programmability and customization. They allow developers to create their own rules, use cases, and functionalities on top of an existing blockchain.

Token Economics and Utility

Tokens often have utility within their respective platforms. They can be used to access premium features, pay for services, or participate in governance decisions. This utility gives tokens inherent value, as they represent something that's useful or valuable within a specific ecosystem.

For example, if you have tokens in a decentralized social media platform, you might use those tokens to boost your posts, tip content creators, or even vote on platform rules and changes.

Token Standards and Their Role in Blockchain Projects

In the previous section, we explored the concept of tokens and how they bring added functionality to the blockchain ecosystem. Now, let's delve into the world of token standards, the most popular being ERC-20 and ERC-721, and how these standards enable diverse use cases within decentralized applications.

Unveiling Token Standards: ERC-20, ERC-721, and More

Token standards are like templates that define how a token should behave on a blockchain. They establish a common set of rules that developers can follow, ensuring compatibility and interoperability between different projects. Let's take a look at two prominent token standards:

ERC-20 Tokens: ERC-20 stands for "Ethereum Request for Comments 20," and it's the most widely used token standard on the Ethereum blockchain. ERC-20 tokens are fungible, meaning each token is interchangeable with another of the same type. These tokens are commonly used for Initial Coin Offerings (ICOs) and in various decentralized applications (DApps).

ERC-721 Tokens: ERC-721, also known as "Non-Fungible Tokens" (NFT), is another token standard on Ethereum. Unlike ERC-20 tokens, each ERC-721 token is unique and can't be exchanged on a one-to-one basis with another token. This uniqueness makes ERC-721 tokens perfect for representing ownership of digital or real-world assets, such as collectibles, artwork, and even real estate.

How Different Token Standards Enable Diverse Use Cases in Decentralized Applications

Token standards play a pivotal role in the functionality of decentralized applications. They define how tokens can be created, transferred, and interacted with. Here are a few examples of how token standards are used in DApps:

- **Gaming:** Many blockchain-based games use ERC-20 and ERC-721 tokens to create in-game items, characters, and virtual assets that players can own, trade, and use within the game environment.

- **Collectibles:** ERC-721 tokens have given rise to the NFT craze, allowing digital artists and creators to tokenize their work as unique pieces of art or collectibles. Each NFT has a distinct value and can be bought, sold, and owned just like physical collectibles.

- **Tokenized Assets:** Real-world assets, such as real estate, can be tokenized using blockchain technology. This means ownership of the asset is represented by a token, making it easier to divide ownership and trade fractions of valuable assets.

- **Decentralized Finance (DeFi):** ERC-20 tokens are the foundation of DeFi platforms, enabling lending, borrowing, yield farming, and more. These tokens create a new financial landscape that's open, transparent, and accessible to anyone with an internet connection.

Real-Life Applications and Future Trends of Tokens

Having explored token standards and their significance in blockchain projects, let's delve into the real-life applications of tokens and explore the exciting trends that are shaping their future.

Tokenization Beyond Cryptocurrencies: Real Assets and Digital Ownership

Tokens are like the digital representation of ownership, and they have the power to transform how we perceive and interact with ownership of both physical and digital assets.

Real Estate Tokenization: Real estate, historically a complex and illiquid investment, can be divided into fractions and tokenized on the blockchain. This allows individuals to invest in properties without the high barriers to entry.

Art and Collectibles: Digital art and collectibles have found a new life with tokens. Artists can tokenize their creations as unique digital assets, giving buyers true ownership and enabling new ways of monetizing digital creativity.

Tokenized Securities: Traditional financial assets like stocks, bonds, and even venture capital investments can be represented as tokens on the blockchain. This opens up the possibility of more efficient trading and ownership transfer.

Emerging Trends and Innovations in Tokenization and Digital Tokens

Tokens are at the forefront of technological innovation and have several exciting trends on the horizon:

DeFi Evolution: Decentralized Finance (DeFi) is expanding beyond its initial offerings. New DeFi projects are experimenting with tokenization of yield-bearing assets, further democratizing access to financial services.

Cross-Chain Interoperability: Different blockchains have their own token standards. Projects are working on solutions that allow tokens to move seamlessly between different blockchains, enhancing interoperability.

Tokenization of Identities: Digital tokens could be used to verify identities securely and privately. This could transform how we prove who we are online while maintaining control over our personal data.

Challenges and Considerations

While the potential of tokens is vast, there are also challenges to navigate:

Regulation: The evolving regulatory landscape affects how tokens can be issued, used, and traded. Clear regulations are essential for the broader adoption of tokenization.

Scalability: As more tokens and projects emerge, scalability becomes a concern. Blockchains need to handle a growing number of transactions without compromising efficiency.

Security: Tokens rely on secure smart contracts and blockchain protocols. Any vulnerabilities can be exploited, leading to loss of funds or assets.

The Future of Tokens: Bridging Digital and Physical Realms

Tokens are shaping a future where ownership and value transfer are borderless and efficient. Whether you're holding a virtual piece of art, a fraction of real estate, or shares in a company, tokens offer a revolutionary way to represent, trade, and engage with ownership.

As technology continues to evolve, tokens will likely become an integral part of our digital and physical lives, transforming industries and creating new economic opportunities. Understanding the power and potential of tokens is essential as we navigate this new era of decentralized ownership and innovation.

What Is Safemoon?

SafeMoon is not your typical cryptocurrency. It's a community driven DeFi (Decentralized Finance) project that's making waves in the crypto world. Here's what you need to know about it:

The Basics: SafeMoon is a DeFi protocol that has over 2.5 million holders and more than $50 million locked in liquidity. It features a unique token called SAFEMOON, which operates on the Binance Smart Chain (BSC). This project started in early 2021 and comes with some interesting features.

Security and Simplicity: While the crypto world offers high returns, it also has its share of challenges, like scams and faulty smart contracts. SafeMoon addresses these issues by adding a high level of security to the DeFi process. It's a community-driven protocol that aims to generate a reasonable yield for investors while automatically managing liquidity and token supply.

The Team: SafeMoon has a dedicated team behind it, including Thomas Smith (CBO), John Karony (CEO), Hank Wyatt (CTO), Jack Haines (COO), Jacob Smith (web developer), and Charles Karony (executive assistant). This team is working hard to make SafeMoon a success.

How SafeMoon Works

SafeMoon operates around its BEP-20 token, SAFEMOON. This token uses a unique mechanism. In every SAFEMOON transaction, there's a 10% fee. Half of this fee (5%) is distributed to

SAFEMOON holders, while the other half (also 5%) is split into two parts. One part is converted into BNB (Binance Coin), and the other part is added to PancakeSwap's liquidity pool. This mechanism rewards people who hold SAFEMOON, and it discourages excessive selling, helping to stabilize the token's price.

Unique Features:

1. Static Rewards: SAFEMOON holders receive 5% of the tokens from every transaction. This helps reduce the selling pressure from early investors and rewards long-term holders.

2. Manual Burn: SafeMoon implements a strategy to burn tokens, reducing the token supply and increasing its value.

3. Automatic Liquidity Pool: A self-sustaining liquidity pool collects tokens from transactions and adds them to SafeMoon's liquidity pool on Pancake Swap. This creates a solid price floor for the token and discourages large-scale selling.

SafeMoon's unique approach to DeFi and its focus on security and simplicity make it stand out in the crypto world. It's a project to keep an eye on if you're interested in the ever-evolving landscape of digital currencies.

Just GOOGLE IT: SAFEMOON REVOLUTION AND FIND SIMILAR TOKENS FOR INVESTMENT

LIST:..

....

....

....

....

....

....

CHAPTER 14 WHAT IS A CRYPTOCURRENCY WALLET?

Types of Cryptocurrency Wallets: Hot Wallets vs. Cold Wallets

Cryptocurrency wallets are like digital safes for your virtual coins. They keep your digital assets secure and accessible, allowing you to send, receive, and manage your cryptocurrencies. There are two main types of wallets: hot wallets and cold wallets. Let's explore each of them and understand how they work.

Hot Wallets: Accessible and Convenient

Hot wallets are like the wallets you carry in your pocket – they're easily accessible and suitable for frequent transactions. These wallets are connected to the internet and can be accessed from various devices, such as your smartphone, tablet, or computer. Here are a few common types of hot wallets:

Online Wallets: These wallets are provided by online cryptocurrency exchanges. They're easy to set up and allow you to access your funds quickly. However, because they're connected to the internet, they're more susceptible to hacking attempts.

Desktop Wallets: These wallets are software applications that you install on your computer. They offer a good balance between accessibility and security. However, if your computer gets infected with malware, your funds could be at risk.

Mobile Wallets: Similar to desktop wallets, mobile wallets are apps that you install on your smartphone. They're convenient for making transactions on the go. Just like online wallets, though, they can be vulnerable to security breaches.

While hot wallets are convenient for everyday use, they carry a higher risk of being hacked due to their constant connection to the internet. Therefore, they're best suited for smaller amounts of cryptocurrency that you're comfortable using for transactions.

Cold Wallets: Maximized Security

Cold wallets, also known as cold storage, offer the highest level of security. They are offline wallets that are not connected to the internet, making them nearly immune to hacking attempts. Cold wallets come in different forms:

Hardware Wallets: These are small physical devices that store your private keys offline. They're considered one of the most secure options. When you want to make a transaction, you connect the hardware wallet to a computer, sign the transaction, and then disconnect it.

Paper Wallets: A paper wallet is a physical piece of paper that contains your private and public keys. It's generated offline and is considered very secure, as long as you keep the paper safe from damage and theft.

Brain Wallets: This unconventional method involves memorizing your private key or passphrase. While it's secure from physical theft, it comes with the risk of forgetting your keys.

Cold wallets are ideal for storing larger amounts of cryptocurrencies for the long term. Since they are offline, they're not susceptible to online attacks. However, it's important to handle them with care and keep them in a safe and secure place.

Choosing the Right Wallet for You

The type of wallet you choose depends on how you plan to use your cryptocurrencies. If you're planning to make frequent transactions, a hot wallet might be more suitable. However, for long-term storage and maximum security, a cold wallet is the way to go.

Best Practices for Keeping Your Crypto Assets Safe

Owning cryptocurrencies is exciting, but it comes with a responsibility to keep your digital assets secure. In this section, we'll explore some essential practices to ensure the safety of your crypto holdings and protect them from potential risks.

- **Choose Strong Passwords and Two-Factor Authentication (2FA)**

Creating strong and unique passwords for your cryptocurrency accounts is the first line of defense. Avoid using easily guessable passwords and consider using a combination of upper and lower-case letters, numbers, and symbols. Additionally, enable Two-Factor Authentication (2FA) wherever possible. 2FA adds an extra layer of security by requiring a second verification step, usually a code sent to your mobile device.

- **Be Cautious with Online Interactions**

Beware of phishing scams and fake websites that try to steal your login information. Always double-check the URL of the website you're visiting, especially when logging in to your cryptocurrency exchange or wallet. Avoid clicking on suspicious links in emails or messages.

- **Regularly Update Software and Devices**

Keep your devices, operating systems, and wallet applications up to date with the latest security patches. Updates often include fixes for known vulnerabilities that hackers could exploit.

- **Backup Your Wallet**

Whether you're using a hot wallet or a cold wallet, regularly back up your wallet's data. This ensures that you can still access your funds if your device is lost or damaged. Store the backup in a safe and secure location.

- **Secure Physical Storage**

If you're using a hardware wallet or a paper wallet, ensure they're stored securely. For hardware wallets, keep them in a safe place away from potential damage or theft. If you're using a paper wallet, consider laminating it to protect it from wear and tear.

- **Diversify and Limit Exposure**

While cryptocurrencies can be a great investment, it's wise to diversify your portfolio. Don't put all your funds into one type of cryptocurrency. This strategy minimizes your risk if one cryptocurrency's value drops significantly.

- **Avoid Public Wi-Fi for Transactions**

Public Wi-Fi networks can be less secure, making your transactions vulnerable to attacks. When making transactions or accessing your wallets, use a secure and private internet connection.

- **Educate Yourself**

Staying informed is your best defense. Learn about common scams, hacking methods, and best practices in the cryptocurrency world. Being aware of potential risks will help you recognize and avoid them.

- **Keep Private Keys Offline**

If you're using a cold wallet, never share your private keys with anyone and keep them offline. Private keys are like the keys to your digital safe; if they fall into the wrong hands, your funds could be stolen.

- **Plan for the Unexpected**

Consider creating a plan for your loved ones to access your crypto holdings in case of unforeseen circumstances. Cryptocurrencies are stored digitally, so without your guidance, your loved ones might not be able to access them.

In conclusion, safeguarding your cryptocurrency assets is of utmost importance in the digital age. By following these best practices, you can significantly reduce the risks associated with owning and managing cryptocurrencies. While the world of cryptocurrencies is exciting, taking the necessary precautions will ensure your journey is both secure and successful.

What Is Trust Wallet?

Secure Your Digital Assets with Trust Wallet

In the ever-expanding world of cryptocurrency, having a secure and reliable cryptocurrency wallet is essential. These wallets are like digital vaults that enable users to send, receive, and store various cryptocurrencies like Bitcoin (BTC), Ether (ETH), and Litecoin (LTC). They come in different forms, such as hardware wallets that resemble USB drives and digital storage options like mobile apps. To ensure the safety of your crypto assets, these wallets use private keys, secret codes that must match a public key for transactions to occur. Trust Wallet is one such secure option.

What Is Trust Wallet?

Trust Wallet is a decentralized and non-custodial multi-cryptocurrency wallet application that gives users full control over their digital assets, including cryptocurrencies and non-fungible tokens (NFTs). It is the official cryptocurrency wallet of Binance, supporting a remarkable 65 blockchains and providing access to over 4.5 million crypto assets.

Unlike centralized wallets, Trust Wallet allows users to interact with decentralized applications (DApps) across supported blockchains, offering a secure and convenient way to explore the world of blockchain-based applications. It aims to make cryptocurrency accessible to everyone by enabling users to buy, send, receive, stake, trade, and store various cryptocurrencies.

One key feature is Trust Wallet's multi-cryptocurrency support. Unlike many wallets that only cater to specific tokens, Trust Wallet offers a wide range of cryptocurrencies, not limited to ERC-20 tokens. Users can easily buy cryptocurrencies through third-party platforms, making the process more flexible. It also functions as an NFT wallet, allowing users to buy, sell, store, and trade NFTs from their mobile devices.

Users can stake selected cryptocurrencies and earn rewards, making their holdings work for them. The wallet offers simple inter-wallet transfers, allowing users to move their assets from other wallets to Trust Wallet using a secret recovery phrase, private key, or Keystore file.

Notably, Trust Wallet is fee-friendly. It's free to use and doesn't charge any subscription fees. While in-app swaps and transactions don't incur additional fees, users are required to pay the corresponding network fees, which can vary depending on network congestion.

How Does Trust Wallet Work?

Trust Wallet acts as a bridge between various blockchains and their respective nodes. Each blockchain has its set of public addresses where cryptocurrencies are encrypted and securely stored. Since Trust Wallet is decentralized and non-custodial, it doesn't hold or control users' cryptocurrency. Instead, it provides users with access to their digital assets.

The Trust Wallet app operates exclusively on mobile devices, making it easy for users to access supported blockchains. The app prioritizes user privacy by not storing any personal information. All contact information is kept private, ensuring that user data is not disclosed to third parties.

One unique feature is the built-in DApp browser, which allows users to access Ethereum-based and BNB Chain-based DApps directly within the Trust Wallet app. Users can interact with DApps without the need for individual sign-ups. Trust Wallet vets all accessible DApps to ensure their trustworthiness and security.

What Can You Do with Trust Wallet?

Trust Wallet offers users a wide range of functionalities beyond just storing cryptocurrencies:

1. Buy Cryptocurrencies: Users can purchase over 60 cryptocurrencies with fiat money using a credit or debit card. They can also buy cryptocurrencies directly from centralized exchanges to reduce card-related fees.

2. Stake Cryptocurrencies: Staking cryptocurrencies from Trust Wallet can lead to interest earnings. Users have various staking options, including BNB and Kava.

Unlocking the Features and Uses of Trust Wallet

Trust Wallet offers a wide range of features and use cases, making it a versatile and user-friendly cryptocurrency wallet.

Flexible Purchases: One of Trust Wallet's standout features is its ability to facilitate the purchase of cryptocurrencies. Users can buy over 60 different cryptocurrencies directly from the app using fiat money through credit or debit cards. This seamless experience makes it easy for both newcomers and experienced traders to acquire digital assets. Moreover, users can also opt to buy cryptocurrencies directly from centralized exchanges, which can help reduce fees associated with card transactions.

Staking and Earning Rewards: Trust Wallet provides users with the opportunity to stake their cryptocurrencies, which can lead to attractive interest earnings. Staking is a way for users to actively participate in network maintenance and governance while being rewarded for their contributions. Among the supported assets for staking on the Trust Wallet app are Binance Coin (BNB) and Kava (KAVA). Staking your holdings can generate passive income and is an appealing feature for those who wish to grow their crypto portfolio.

User-Friendly Inter-Wallet Transfers: Transferring cryptocurrencies between wallets is made easy with Trust Wallet. Users can seamlessly move their digital assets from other wallets to Trust Wallet using a secret recovery phrase, private key, or Keystore file. This simplifies the process of consolidating your crypto holdings and centralizing them within Trust Wallet for easier management.

Cost-Effective Usage: Trust Wallet offers a cost-effective approach to managing cryptocurrencies. While the app itself is free to use and doesn't impose any subscription fees, it's important to note that Trust Wallet doesn't charge additional fees for in-app swaps or transactions. However, users are required to pay the corresponding network fees, which can vary based on network congestion. This fee structure ensures that Trust Wallet remains a budget-friendly choice for crypto enthusiasts.

Secure Access to DApps: Trust Wallet's built-in DApp browser allows users to access decentralized applications (DApps) on the Ethereum and BNB Chain networks. This feature makes it easy for users to explore and interact with a wide range of DApps without the need for separate accounts or sign-ups. Trust Wallet takes an extra step by carefully vetting DApps to ensure that only trustworthy and secure options are made available to its users. Among the supported DApps are popular platforms like Uniswap, PancakeSwap, and OpenSea.

CHAPTER 15 WHAT IS ICO?

Understanding ICOs and How They Fund Projects

In recent years, Initial Coin Offerings (ICOs) have taken the world of fundraising by storm, offering a new way for projects and startups to gather funds for their ventures. ICOs leverage the power of cryptocurrencies and blockchain technology to democratize the investment landscape. In this section, we'll dive into the fascinating world of ICOs and how they function as a crowdfunding revolution.

The Concept of ICOs

Imagine you have a brilliant idea for a new technology, platform, or service, but you need funds to bring your vision to life. Traditionally, you might seek investors who are willing to provide capital in exchange for ownership or shares in your project. However, ICOs introduce a new paradigm.

In an ICO, instead of selling ownership stakes, projects issue their own digital tokens. These tokens represent a form of value within the project's ecosystem. Investors who participate in the ICO purchase these tokens using cryptocurrencies like Bitcoin or Ethereum.

How ICOs Fund Projects

ICOs allow projects to raise funds from a global pool of investors without the intermediaries of traditional financial systems. Here's how the process generally works:

Whitepaper: The project team prepares a detailed whitepaper that outlines the project's goals, technology, use cases for the token, and how the funds raised will be used to develop the project.

Token Creation: The project creates a new cryptocurrency token using blockchain technology. This token will serve as a digital asset that investors can purchase.

Token Sale: During the ICO, investors can buy the project's tokens using established cryptocurrencies like Bitcoin or Ethereum. The price of the tokens and the number of tokens issued are usually determined before the ICO begins.

Funds Allocation: The funds raised through the ICO are used to develop the project, create the intended technology or platform, and cover operational costs.

Token Utilization: As the project develops, the tokens can be used within the platform or ecosystem the project aims to create. They might represent access to services, voting rights, digital goods, or other forms of value.

Advantages of ICOs

ICOs have several advantages that have contributed to their popularity:

Global Reach: Anyone with an internet connection and cryptocurrency can participate in ICOs, allowing projects to tap into a worldwide pool of potential investors.

Accessibility: ICOs provide an opportunity for individuals who might not have access to traditional investment avenues to invest in promising projects.

Innovation: ICOs have fueled the development of countless innovative projects, ranging from blockchain platforms to decentralized applications.

Challenges and Concerns

While ICOs offer exciting possibilities, they also come with their fair share of challenges and concerns:

Lack of Regulation: The lack of comprehensive regulations in the ICO space has led to instances of fraudulent projects and scams.

Volatility: Cryptocurrency markets can be highly volatile, and this volatility can affect the value of tokens purchased during an ICO.

Due Diligence: Investors need to thoroughly research projects before participating in ICOs to ensure they are legitimate and have a solid plan.

Risks and Considerations for ICO Investors

As exciting as Initial Coin Offerings (ICOs) are, it's crucial to understand that they come with risks. While ICOs offer opportunities for individuals to invest in innovative projects, it's essential to approach them with caution and careful consideration. In this section, we'll explore the potential risks and important factors that potential ICO investors should keep in mind.

Lack of Regulation and Scams

One of the biggest challenges with ICOs is the lack of regulatory oversight. Unlike traditional investment markets, the ICO space is still evolving, and there are fewer safeguards in place. This lack of regulation has led to instances of fraudulent projects and scams, where individuals create fake projects to deceive investors and disappear with their funds.

Volatility and Market Fluctuations

Cryptocurrencies, including the tokens purchased during ICOs, can be highly volatile. The value of tokens can fluctuate dramatically in a short period, leading to potential losses for investors. It's essential to be prepared for these market fluctuations and invest only what you can afford to lose.

Unrealistic Expectations

Some projects overpromise and underdeliver. They might make

grand claims about their technology, potential returns, or utility of their tokens. It's crucial to carefully evaluate the claims made by a project and assess whether they are realistic and achievable.

Lack of Transparency

The success of an ICO depends on the credibility and transparency of the project team. If a project lacks a clear roadmap, a comprehensive whitepaper, or a transparent team background, it could be a red flag. It's essential to research the team's qualifications, the project's goals, and how the raised funds will be used.

Potential for Losing Private Keys

When you participate in an ICO, you'll receive tokens in your cryptocurrency wallet. It's crucial to securely store your private keys and back up your wallet. Losing your private keys means losing access to your tokens forever.

Technological Challenges and Delays

Blockchain and cryptocurrency projects are complex and require significant technical expertise. Delays in development or technological challenges could impact the project's timeline and potential success.

Important Considerations for ICO Investors

Do Your Research: Thoroughly research the project, its technology, team, and roadmap. Look for credible sources of information and seek reviews from experts in the field.

Understand the Use Case: Understand the purpose of the token within the project's ecosystem. Does it solve a real-world problem? Is there demand for the token's utility?

Assess the Team: Evaluate the project team's expertise, experience, and track record. A strong team increases the project's chances of success.

Check for Regulatory Compliance: Ensure that the project is compliant with any applicable regulations in the region where it operates.

Invest What You Can Afford to Lose: Due to the inherent risks and market volatility, only invest an amount you can afford to lose without affecting your financial well-being.

Diversify Your Portfolio: Avoid putting all your funds into a single ICO. Diversifying your investments reduces the impact of potential losses.

I THINK BITCOIN IS ON THE VERGE OF GETTING BROAD ACCEPTANCE BY CONVENTIONAL FINANCE PEOPLE."

ELON MUSK

CHAPTER 16 MAJOR CRYPTO SCAMS?

Scammers appear to have existed since the dawn of time. At least since recorded history began. There appears to be an increase in frauds with each new discovery and technology. Cryptography is no exception. With the emergence of bitcoin, it became clear how simple it was to duplicate reputable companies' open-source code and create new cryptocurrencies. Some of these were and continue to be excellent.

98% of ICOs — the thousands of new cryptocurrencies launched by initial coin offerings during the 2016-2018 crypto bubble – were later discovered to be either scams or massive failures.

Onecoin - popularised by the BBC's Missing Crypto queen podcast series, Onecoin is now widely regarded as the largest cryptocurrency hoax of all time. The Onecoin hoax, now acknowledged to be a massive Ponzi scheme, is thought to have stolen an estimated $25 billion. Despite authorities shutting down the scam in 2017, arresting its leaders and disappearing - on the run or dead - the scheme is still operating. Most bizarrely, Onecoin never had a cryptocurrency; the technology was a sham from the start.

Bitconnect - another of the most audacious and well-known cryptocurrency frauds of all time. Bitconnect defrauded investors out of an estimated $4 billion in a multi-level marketing-led Ponzi scheme, drawing them in with claims of an unbeatable trading algorithm that, perhaps obviously, never existed. Surprisingly, they weren't satisfied with only duping their victims once, creating a second fraudulent ICO, BitconnectX, just as their first business was failing.

Bit club Network is the most well-known cryptocurrency mining fraud. This, like Onecoin and Bitconnect, was a Ponzi scheme that leveraged clever marketing and salespeople to pull in $722 million. BCN told its investors that it would deliver them guaranteed returns if they purchased bitcoin mining equipment. Unfortunately, the mining equipment films it used belonged to another mining farm, and it appears to have been a Ponzi scheme from start to finish.

Quadriga - the cryptocurrency exchange whose founder is infamously thought to have faked his own death - was once Canada's largest and trusted cryptocurrency exchange. However, it was eventually discovered that it had been conducted fraudulently from the start, and its creators were skilled in operating numerous scams. The founder was the only one with access to the private keys containing C$250 million in cryptocurrency belonging to its customers when he mysteriously died, except that most don't believe he died, and some are still clamouring for his body to be excavated to obtain proof.

Pin coin and iFan are two Vietnamese projects that used convincing sales events and creative marketing to defraud $660 million from their investors. Much of this cryptocurrency remains unaccounted for.

Plex coin - an ICO that, astonishingly, guaranteed 1,354% returns to investors before being shut down by the SEC and required to reimburse $20 million it had stolen.

Savedroid - not a scam in and of itself, but its owners locked down their office and social media before tactfully posed in an airport and on a beach pretending to have been exit scammed before returning to clarify it wasn't a hoax. In any case, the project's tokens plummeted in value, costing investors more than $50 million because of the deception.

Thodex - With offers of free memecoin Doge, the founder of this Turkish crypto exchange enticed investors to deposit $2.2 billion of their crypto on his exchange before leaving scamming with the lot. It is still unknown where he is.

Did you Know?

Pizza was the first commercial bitcoin transaction.

A man in Florida spent 10,000 bitcoins (BTC) for two pizzas on May 22, 2010. This is widely acknowledged as the first commercial Bitcoin transaction.

At the time, 10,000 bitcoins were valued at around $40, making one bitcoin worth just under half a cent. You'd be a Bitcoin millionaire if you owned that many Bitcoins in September 2023. 10,000 bitcoins are worth more than $290 million in the market.

CHAPTER 17 NAVIGATING REGULATORY CHALLENGES

Navigating regulatory challenges for cryptocurrency is a complex and dynamic task that requires understanding the different types of crypto assets, the existing and emerging laws and regulations in various jurisdictions, and the potential risks and benefits of crypto innovation. Some of the main challenges include:

- **Defining and classifying crypto** assets based on their technological features, functions, and use cases. Crypto assets can range from cryptocurrencies like Bitcoin and Ethereum to stablecoins that are pegged to fiat currencies or other assets, utility tokens that provide access to a service or platform, to security tokens that represent ownership or rights in an underlying asset or entity. Different types of crypto assets may have different legal implications and regulatory requirements.

- **Balancing innovation and consumer protection.** Crypto innovation can offer new opportunities for financial inclusion, efficiency, transparency, and competition, but it can also pose risks such as fraud, money laundering, tax evasion, cyberattacks, market volatility, and environmental impact. Regulators need to find ways to foster a conducive environment for crypto innovation while safeguarding the interests and rights of consumers and investors.

- **Coordinating with other regulators and stakeholders.** Crypto regulation is not a one-size-fits-all approach, as different countries and regions have different legal systems, financial markets, and policy objectives. Regulators need to collaborate with each other and with the crypto industry, academia, civil society, and international organizations to harmonize standards, avoid regulatory arbitrage, and promote a globally consistent framework for crypto governance.

The global regulatory landscape for cryptocurrencies is still evolving and varies widely across countries and regions. Some of the main trends and developments are:

- **The emergence of crypto-friendly jurisdictions.** Some countries have adopted a proactive and supportive stance towards crypto innovation, providing clear and comprehensive regulations, tax incentives, sandbox programs, and digital infrastructure for crypto businesses and users. Examples include Singapore, Switzerland, Malta, Estonia, Japan, South Korea, and the UK.

- **The crackdown on crypto activities.** Some countries have taken a restrictive and hostile approach towards crypto innovation, banning or limiting crypto activities, imposing strict regulations and sanctions, or creating barriers for crypto businesses and users.

Examples include China, India, Russia, Turkey, Iran, Nigeria, and Algeria.

- **The exploration of central bank digital currencies (CBDCs).** Many central banks are researching or developing their own digital currencies that are issued and backed by the state. CBDCs aim to provide a secure, efficient, and inclusive alternative to cash and other payment methods. Some countries have already launched or piloted their CBDCs, such as China's digital yuan, the Bahamas' sand dollar, Sweden's e-krona, and Ukraine's e-hryvnia.

How regulations impact crypto users and businesses depends on the type of regulation, the type of crypto asset, the type of activity, and the jurisdiction involved. Some of the possible impacts are:

- **Compliance costs and obligations.** Crypto users and businesses may need to comply with various regulations such as registration, licensing, reporting, disclosure, auditing, taxation, anti-money laundering (AML), know your customer (KYC), consumer protection, data privacy, cybersecurity, etc. These may entail additional costs and obligations that could affect their profitability and competitiveness.

- **Legal certainty and protection.** Crypto users and businesses may benefit from clear and consistent regulations that provide legal certainty and protection for their rights and interests. This could enhance their confidence and trust in the crypto sector and reduce the risks of disputes or litigation.

-

- **Access and participation.** Crypto users and businesses may face different levels of access and participation in the crypto sector depending on the regulations in place. Some regulations may facilitate or encourage access and participation by providing incentives or removing barriers for crypto activities. Other regulations may restrict or discourage access and participation by imposing penalties or prohibitions for crypto activities.

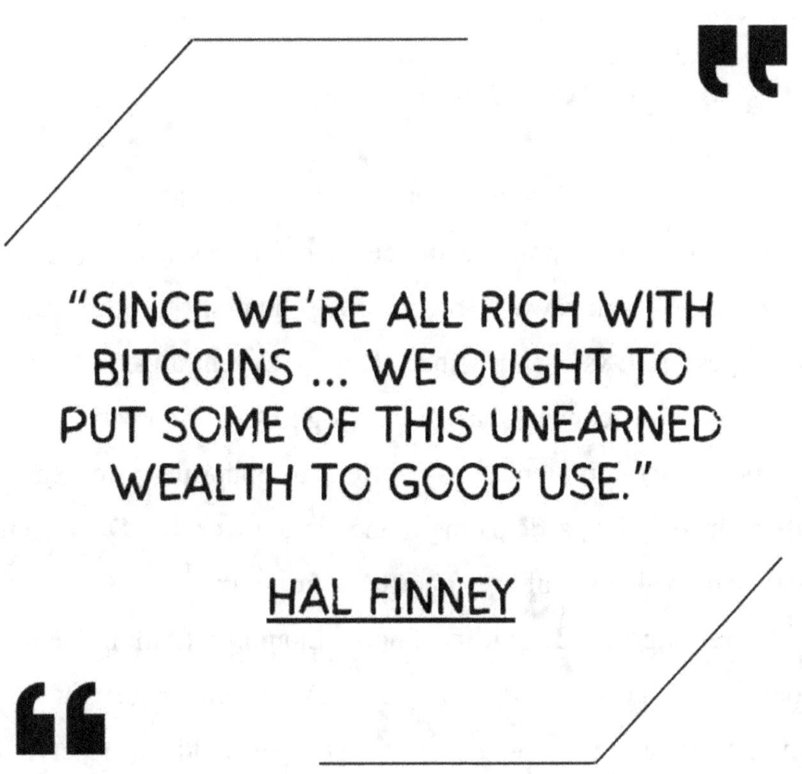

CHAPTER 18 FARMING AND STACKING IN CRYPTO

Cryptocurrency Farming

Cryptocurrency farming, also known as liquidity farming or yield farming, is a practice in the blockchain space that allows individuals to earn rewards by providing liquidity to decentralized exchanges (DEXs) and other DeFi (Decentralized Finance) platforms. This concept has gained significant popularity in the cryptocurrency community, as it offers an opportunity to generate passive income by participating in the vibrant world of DeFi. Here's a detailed breakdown of cryptocurrency farming:

Understanding Liquidity Pools: Liquidity farming revolves around the concept of liquidity pools. A liquidity pool is a smart contract on a decentralized exchange that holds a reserve of cryptocurrency tokens, usually in pairs. For instance, a common pair in DeFi is ETH (Ethereum) and DAI (a stablecoin). Users contribute an equal value of both tokens to the pool, creating liquidity for trading.

How Cryptocurrency Farming Works: Farming begins with a user providing liquidity to a specific liquidity pool. This usually involves depositing an equal value of two different tokens into the pool. For example, a user might deposit $1,000 worth of ETH and $1,000 worth of DAI into an ETH-DAI liquidity pool.

Once a user has provided liquidity, they receive a liquidity provider (LP) token as proof of their stake in the pool. These LP tokens represent the user's share of the pool.

Farming rewards are distributed in the form of tokens native to the DeFi project or exchange where liquidity is provided. These rewards are proportionate to the user's share of the liquidity pool, which is determined by the number of LP tokens they hold. In most cases, the rewards are issued periodically and automatically.

Risk and Considerations

Farming can be lucrative, but it's not without risks. The key risks include:

- **Impermanent Loss**: When prices of the tokens in the liquidity pool change, you may experience impermanent loss, which can result in reduced earnings.

- **Smart Contract Risks**: DeFi platforms rely on smart

contracts, and there have been instances of exploits and vulnerabilities, which can lead to the loss of funds.

- **Volatility**: The tokens you deposit can be highly volatile, potentially affecting your overall profitability.

Cryptocurrency Staking

Cryptocurrency staking is a method of participating in a blockchain network's proof-of-stake (PoS) consensus mechanism to secure the network and earn rewards. Unlike traditional proof-of-work (PoW) systems that require mining, staking is more energy-efficient and accessible to a broader audience. Here's an in-depth look at cryptocurrency staking:

Understanding Proof-of-Stake: To grasp staking, it's essential to understand PoS, the consensus mechanism. In PoS, validators are chosen to create new blocks and validate transactions based on the amount of cryptocurrency they "stake" as collateral.

How Cryptocurrency Staking Works: Staking involves "locking up" a certain amount of cryptocurrency in a wallet designated for staking. The more cryptocurrency you stake, the higher your chances of being selected as a validator to create new blocks and validate transactions.

In return for providing this service to the network, stakers receive rewards, typically in the form of the network's native cryptocurrency. These rewards are distributed periodically, and the staker can choose to re-stake them, thus compounding their earnings.

Staking is generally viewed as a more passive and less resource-intensive method of participating in blockchain networks compared to mining in PoW systems.

Risk and Considerations

While staking is generally considered lower risk than other cryptocurrency activities, there are some important considerations:

Slashing Risk: Validators can face penalties (slashing) if they behave maliciously or negligently, which can result in the loss of a portion of their staked funds.

Token Volatility: The value of the staked cryptocurrency can fluctuate, affecting the overall value of the staked assets.

Lock-Up Period: Some networks may require a lock-up period, during which you cannot access your staked assets.

Key Differences and Benefits of Farming and Staking

Now, let's compare farming and staking to highlight their key differences and benefits:

1. Purpose:

- **Farming:** Provides liquidity to DEXs and DeFi platforms, allowing users to earn rewards in the form of project tokens and fees.

- **Staking:** Secures a blockchain network and validators earn rewards in the network's native cryptocurrency.

2. Risk Profile:

- **Farming:** Can be riskier due to potential impermanent loss and smart contract risks.

- **Staking:** Generally considered less risky, with a lower likelihood of losing staked funds.

3. Tokens Received:

- **Farming:** Rewards are often project-specific tokens and trading fees.

- **Staking:** Rewards are usually in the same cryptocurrency that is staked.

4. Liquidity Involvement:

- **Farming:** Requires users to provide liquidity by depositing tokens into a pool.

- **Staking:** Involves simply locking up a set number of tokens.

5. Passive Income:

- **Farming:** Offers the potential for passive income through yield generation.

- **Staking:** Provides a steady source of passive income for securing a network.

In conclusion, both farming and staking offer opportunities to earn rewards in the cryptocurrency space. The choice between the two depends on your risk tolerance, investment goals, and the specific project or network you're interested in. It's crucial to conduct thorough research and consider the risks and rewards associated with each before participating.

What is Pancake Swap (CAKE)?

PancakeSwap is a leading decentralized exchange (DEX) and automated market maker (AMM) that operates on the Binance Smart Chain (BSC). It stands out for offering lower transaction costs compared to Ethereum-based platforms. PancakeSwap provides a wide range of DeFi services, including trading, staking, liquidity provision, and even NFTs, all powered by smart contracts.

As of October 2022, PancakeSwap dominates the DeFi landscape on the Binance Smart Chain, accounting for more than 50% of DeFi activity. Its user-friendly interface allows anyone to connect their wallets and trade in a non-custodial manner.

The total value locked (TVL) in staking on PancakeSwap has exceeded $4 billion as of October 2022. The platform boasts over 1.9 million users who have executed more than 22 million trades in September 2022 alone.

PancakeSwap's native cryptocurrency is the BEP20 token

known as CAKE. This token serves as the utility coin for the PancakeSwap DEX and offers a wide range of uses, including liquidity mining rewards, lottery participation, governance, trading fee discounts, and more.

How Does PancakeSwap Work?

PancakeSwap is a decentralized application (dApp) built on the Binance Smart Chain (BSC). The platform empowers users to perform three core functions:

1. Trade: PancakeSwap enables users to seamlessly swap one cryptocurrency for another using its intuitive interface. What sets it apart is its lower transaction fees, thanks to the BSC's efficiency, making PancakeSwap a cost-effective choice compared to Ethereum-based DEXs.

2. Earn: Staking CAKE tokens on PancakeSwap opens up avenues for users to earn attractive returns on their crypto holdings. The platform provides multiple options, including Syrup Pools for staking CAKE, yield farms where LP tokens can be staked to earn CAKE, and even the ability to earn trading fees by staking tokens in Liquidity Pools (LPs).

3. Win: PancakeSwap introduces various rewarding features to keep users engaged. This includes lotteries and NFT collectibles, as well as the opportunity to participate in predicting the price changes of BNB. Additionally, the platform offers lock-staking and Pottery lotteries, giving users the chance to maximize their yields on CAKE deposits.

History of PancakeSwap and $CAKE

PancakeSwap was launched on the Binance Smart Chain in September 2020 as a response to the network congestion and high gas fees faced by Ethereum-based DEXs. It was developed by anonymous creators.

Within a remarkably short span of time, by February 2021, PancakeSwap became the first Binance Smart Chain project to reach a valuation of $1 billion. In April 2021, Version 2 of the platform was rolled out, introducing additional features and capabilities.

In the same month, PancakeSwap introduced Initial Farm Offerings (IFOs), a mechanism for new projects to raise funds via its platform. A seed round in July 2021 saw the team behind PancakeSwap secure $4 million in funding.

In Q1 2022, PancakeSwap launched a service that allowed users to buy and sell third-party BSC NFTs on its platform. The roadmap for subsequent periods includes perpetuals trading, fixed-term staking, limit orders, NFT utility, NFT-based gamification, hackathons, a new version of the Lottery, and an affiliate system.

Throughout Q2 and Q3 2022, PancakeSwap continued to work on enhancing its prediction feature, expanding support for multiple currencies, and implementing various upgrades across the platform, including IFOs, voting mechanisms, NFT markets, and staking enhancements.

CHAPTER 19 THE METAVERSE: BEYOND VIRTUAL REALITY, A NEW DIGITAL FRONTIER

The term "metaverse" is buzzing across the digital realm and quickly becoming more than just a futuristic concept. It's a technological phenomenon that's reshaping how we interact with the digital world and each other. The metaverse represents a collective virtual shared space, merging physical reality and the digital realm, where people can seamlessly interact, socialize, and explore boundless virtual environments. In this article, we will delve into what the metaverse is, how it works, and its implications for our future.

Defining the Metaverse

The metaverse is a vast digital universe composed of interconnected virtual worlds, where people can create, socialize, work, play, and explore. It's an expansive ecosystem of interconnected digital spaces and environments that allows for persistent, shared experiences. Unlike traditional online spaces, the metaverse strives for continuity and unity. Instead of multiple isolated applications or websites, users navigate through a singular, seamless universe, much like moving from room to room in a physical space.

The metaverse concept has roots in science fiction, most notably in Neal Stephenson's 1992 novel "Snow Crash," where the term was first coined. Since then, it has evolved from fiction into a rapidly developing digital reality.

Key Elements of the Metaverse

Digital Twin of Reality: The metaverse mirrors the physical world in many ways. It consists of 3D virtual spaces, digital replicas of real-world locations, and entirely imaginary environments. This digital twin provides a space for human interaction and creativity.

User-Generated Content: In the metaverse, users can create and modify the environment. They design avatars, objects, and spaces, shaping the metaverse's development. This user-generated content fosters a sense of ownership and engagement.

Interconnectedness: One of the defining features is the interconnected nature of the metaverse. Users can traverse different digital spaces with their avatars. This facilitates communication, collaboration, and shared experiences across various virtual realms.

Blockchain and Digital Assets: The metaverse relies on blockchain technology for security, ownership, and transfer of digital assets. Users can own unique digital assets and currency, which can be traded or sold both within and outside the metaverse.

Economy and Work: People engage in economic activities within the metaverse, including virtual businesses, digital real estate, and creative work. Some users earn their livelihood exclusively within these virtual spaces.

Metaverse in Action

The metaverse isn't limited to a single platform; it encompasses numerous digital spaces and platforms. Some notable examples include:

Roblox: This gaming platform allows users to create, play, and monetize their games, creating a thriving virtual economy.

Decentraland: It's a blockchain-based virtual world where users buy, develop, and sell parcels of digital real estate. Here, they can host events, socialize, and even open businesses.

Facebook Horizon: Facebook's venture into the metaverse promises a social virtual reality platform where users can create, socialize, and attend events.

CryptoKitties: This blockchain-based game lets users collect, breed, and trade virtual cats. Each cat is a unique digital asset.

Implications and Challenges

The metaverse's potential is vast, ranging from transforming entertainment and social interactions to redefining work and education. However, it also raises significant concerns. Privacy, security, and digital addiction are critical issues. Moreover, the metaverse's ownership and control are questions that must be addressed. It's an evolving concept that will require collective effort to shape its future.

In summary, the metaverse represents a convergence of technology, digital culture, and human interaction. It's a digital frontier where the boundaries between reality and the virtual world blur. As it continues to expand, it holds both promise and challenges for our increasingly interconnected digital society.

The Sandbox (SAND) Crypto: Where Creativity Meets the Blockchain

The Sandbox is a virtual metaverse, and SAND is the cryptocurrency that powers this digital realm. In The Sandbox, users become creators, owners, and entrepreneurs, shaping their virtual experiences within a blockchain-based ecosystem. Let's dive into how it all works.

Creating Virtual Worlds

The Sandbox is all about creation. Users can craft and design their virtual gaming experiences, unleashing their creativity. From game levels to interactive environments, you're in control.

Ownership through NFTs

Ownership in The Sandbox is established through Non-Fungible Tokens (NFTs). Specifically, digital parcels of land known as LAND are represented as NFTs on the Ethereum blockchain. When you own LAND, you gain creative rights and control within the metaverse.

Monetizing Creations and Experiences

In The Sandbox, you can turn your digital creations into real assets. Whether it's your LAND parcels or in-game assets, you can sell or trade these NFTs for SAND or other cryptocurrencies. This monetization potential has created a thriving economy within the metaverse.

Community-Driven Ecosystem: The Sandbox thrives on decentralization and community involvement. Creators are empowered to design, share, and sell in-world assets, fostering a dynamic and vibrant ecosystem where innovation knows no bounds.

A Glimpse into the Past

The Sandbox's journey is a fascinating evolution from a video game to a blockchain-based metaverse:

2011 - Pixowl Founded: It all started with the founding of Pixowl by Arthur Madrid and Sebastien Borget. Pixowl played a pivotal role in developing The Sandbox game.

2012 - Video Game Launch: In 2012, The Sandbox emerged as a video game. It quickly gained popularity, with a staggering 40 million mobile device downloads.

January 2018 - Blockchain Version Development: The true transformation began in January 2018 when The Sandbox started developing its blockchain version on the Ethereum blockchain. This shift marked a significant turning point, steering the project from a traditional video game to a blockchain-based metaverse.

The blockchain transition opened a world of opportunities. The Sandbox now offers a 3D, multiplayer format where users can unleash their creativity, own digital land, and monetize their gaming experiences. This transformation has not only redefined entertainment within the platform but has also created exciting monetization prospects for its users.

The Sandbox stands at the intersection of innovation, creativity, and blockchain technology, promising new possibilities for virtual worlds and digital economies.

Decentraland (MANA) Crypto: Unveiling a Decentralized Virtual Universe

Decentraland is not just another virtual world; it's an entirely decentralized metaverse governed by a decentralized autonomous organization (DAO). Within this digital realm, you'll find innovation, blockchain, and MANA, the native cryptocurrency that fuels it all. So, what's the story behind Decentraland and how does this decentralized metaverse work?

Creating Immersive Worlds with MANA

Decentraland offers a shared virtual world where users can engage in immersive games, socialize, connect with businesses, and even find investment opportunities. The entire metaverse is built on the Ethereum blockchain, and MANA serves as its native cryptocurrency.

Here's how it works:

Digital Land Ownership

Users can buy digital parcels of land, known as LAND, which are represented as Non-Fungible Tokens (NFTs). These NFTs give users creative rights and ownership within the metaverse. Think of it as owning a piece of the digital universe.

Monetizing the Virtual Experience

LANDowners can monetize their virtual real estate by developing and expanding their digital lands into districts. All transactions within Decentraland, whether for buying, selling, or trading, require MANA. It's the lifeblood of this decentralized universe.

Accessibility and Monetization

To get into Decentraland, users can easily sign up via web browsers. By linking a digital wallet, they can fully immerse themselves in this digital realm, hold MANA, buy, and sell LAND NFTs, and collect various digital collectibles.

The Evolution of Decentraland and MANA Coin

The journey of Decentraland and its native cryptocurrency, MANA, has been an exciting one:

Founders and Early Vision: The co-founders, Ariel Meilich and Esteban Ordano, initially envisioned a proof of concept, known as Decentraland's Stone Age, showcasing the potential of blockchain technology in digital real estate ownership.

The Bronze Age: Transitioning from 2D, Decentraland entered the Bronze Age in late 2016. This introduced a 3D virtual world made up of land parcels.

The Iron Age: The Iron Age expanded Decentraland's horizons, incorporating social elements and creating a more content-rich environment. It also opened doors for decentralized applications (dApps) within Decentraland, allowing developers to craft unique experiences.

Genesis City and Marketplace: In December 2017, LAND tokens associated with Genesis City were auctioned, introducing the concept of virtual land ownership. In March 2018, the Decentraland Marketplace made it possible to buy and sell LAND parcels within Genesis City.

A Thriving Metaverse: In January 2020, Decentral and's dream became a reality as the metaverse went live. Users found themselves immersed in a decentralized, Ethereum-based virtual world, teeming with opportunities.

Decentraland's journey underscores the potential of blockchain technology to reshape digital experiences. With MANA at its core, Decentraland provides a secure and engaging ecosystem where users can create, explore, socialize, and even find economic opportunities within this boundary-pushing digital universe.

Emerging Trends and Innovations in the Crypto Space

The crypto space is a rapidly evolving and exciting field with a lot of potential for innovation and disruption. Some of the emerging trends and innovations that are likely to shape the future direction of the industry are:

Decentralized finance (DeFi): DeFi is a term that refers to a range of financial services and applications that are built on decentralized platforms, such as blockchain and smart contracts. DeFi aims to provide more accessible, transparent, efficient, and inclusive alternatives to traditional financial intermediaries and systems. Some examples of DeFi applications include lending and borrowing platforms, decentralized exchanges, stablecoins, yield farming, insurance, prediction markets, and more. DeFi has grown exponentially in the past year, reaching over $100 billion in total value locked as of September 2021.

Blockchain technology innovation: The use of blockchain technology in other industries beyond finance is also a trend that is likely to gain traction in the future. Blockchain technology can offer benefits such as immutability, transparency, security, traceability, and automation for various use cases and sectors. Some examples of blockchain technology innovation include supply chain management, digital identity, healthcare, gaming, art, social media, and more. Blockchain technology is also constantly evolving and improving, with new developments such as layer-2 solutions, interoperability protocols, privacy-enhancing techniques, and quantum-resistant algorithms.

Gaming: An exciting area of growth in the cryptocurrency space is in the gaming industry. Gaming and crypto have a natural synergy, as both involve digital assets, virtual worlds, online communities, and incentives. Crypto gaming experiences and abilities for gamers, such as owning and trading their in-game items, earning rewards for playing or creating games, accessing cross-platform and cross-game experiences, and participating in decentralized governance. Some examples of crypto gaming platforms include Axie Infinity, Decentraland, The Sandbox, and Enjin.

Potential Challenges and the Road Ahead

Despite the promising opportunities and innovations that cryptocurrencies offer, there are also significant challenges and risks that need to be addressed and overcome. Some of the potential challenges and the road ahead for cryptocurrencies are:

Environmental impact: The environmental impact of cryptocurrencies, especially those that use proof-of-work consensus mechanisms such as Bitcoin and Ethereum, has been a major concern for many stakeholders. Cryptocurrencies can consume a lot of energy and generate high levels of carbon emissions due to the intensive computational processes involved in mining and validating transactions. According to an index compiled by the University of Cambridge, Bitcoin mining alone accounts for about 0.5% of global electricity consumption as of September 2021. There are several initiatives and solutions that aim to reduce or mitigate the environmental impact of cryptocurrencies, such as switching to more energy-efficient consensus mechanisms (e.g., proof-of-stake), using renewable energy sources or carbon offsets, improving mining efficiency and hardware design, and developing green blockchain standards and certifications.

Regulatory uncertainty: The regulatory landscape for cryptocurrencies is still evolving and varies widely across countries and regions. Some countries have adopted a proactive and supportive stance towards crypto innovation, providing clear and comprehensive regulations, tax incentives, sandbox programs, and digital infrastructure for crypto businesses and users. Examples include Singapore, Switzerland, Malta, Estonia, Japan, South Korea, and the UK. Some countries have taken a restrictive and hostile approach towards crypto innovation, banning, or limiting crypto activities, imposing strict regulations and sanctions, or creating barriers for crypto businesses and users. Examples include China, India, Russia, Turkey, Iran, Nigeria, and Algeria. Some countries have taken a cautious or ambivalent approach towards crypto innovation, allowing, or tolerating some crypto activities but without providing clear or consistent regulations or guidance for crypto businesses and users. Examples include the US, Canada, Australia, New Zealand, Brazil, South Africa, and Thailand. The regulatory uncertainty creates challenges for crypto businesses and users in terms of compliance costs, legal risks,

Regulatory uncertainty (continued): The regulatory uncertainty creates challenges for crypto businesses and users in terms of compliance costs, legal risks, market access, and innovation potential. Regulators need to balance innovation and consumer protection, coordinate with other regulators and stakeholders, and promote a globally consistent framework for crypto governance.

Security and scalability: The security and scalability of cryptocurrencies are also important issues that need to be addressed and improved. Cryptocurrencies are vulnerable to various types of cyberattacks, such as hacking, phishing, malware, denial-of-service, 51% attacks, and more. These attacks can compromise the integrity, availability, and confidentiality of the crypto networks and assets, resulting in losses, disruptions, or frauds. Cryptocurrencies also face scalability challenges, such as limited transaction throughput, high transaction fees, network congestion, and long confirmation times. These challenges can affect the performance, usability, and adoption of cryptosystems and services. There are several initiatives and solutions that aim to enhance the security and scalability of cryptocurrencies, such as implementing better security practices and standards, developing more robust and resilient protocols and platforms, adopting layer-2 solutions, or sharing techniques, and leveraging artificial intelligence or quantum computing.

CHAPTER 20 CRYPTOCURRENCY AND THE ECONOMY

The Impact of Digital Money on Traditional Financial Systems

The rise of cryptocurrencies has introduced a new and revolutionary form of digital money that has the potential to disrupt traditional financial systems. In this section, we'll explore how cryptocurrencies are impacting these systems and reshaping the way we think about money and transactions.

Decentralization and Financial Empowerment:

Cryptocurrencies, like Bitcoin, operate on decentralized blockchain technology. This means that transactions are verified and recorded by a distributed network of computers, removing the need for a central authority like a bank. This decentralization gives individuals more control over their funds and transactions, empowering them to be their own banks.

Borderless Transactions

Traditional financial systems often involve intermediaries and can be slow and expensive for cross-border transactions. Cryptocurrencies enable instant and borderless transactions, eliminating the need for intermediaries like banks and reducing transaction fees. This has significant implications for international trade and remittances.

Financial Inclusion

A large portion of the global population lacks access to traditional banking services. Cryptocurrencies have the potential to bridge this gap by providing financial services to the unbanked and underbanked populations. With just a smartphone and internet access, individuals can access the world of digital finance.

Challenges to Traditional Banking

As more people adopt cryptocurrencies, traditional banks face challenges in retaining customers. Individuals who value the autonomy and lower fees offered by cryptocurrencies may choose to move away from traditional banking systems.

Central Bank Digital Currencies (CBDCs)

Some countries are exploring the development of their own digital currencies, known as Central Bank Digital Currencies (CBDCs). These digital versions of national currencies could coexist with traditional cash and provide governments with more direct control over monetary policy and transactions.

The Role of Financial Institutions

While cryptocurrencies challenge traditional financial systems, they have also prompted financial institutions to explore blockchain technology and digital asset offerings. Some banks are considering ways to integrate cryptocurrencies into their services.

Regulatory Challenges

The rise of cryptocurrencies has posed regulatory challenges for governments around the world. Balancing innovation and consumer protection while preventing illegal activities like money laundering is a complex task.

Speculation and Volatility

Cryptocurrencies are known for their price volatility, which can lead to speculative trading. While this volatility can present investment opportunities, it also introduces risks for investors and challenges for traditional economic stability.

Adoption and Acceptance of Cryptocurrency in Different Countries

Cryptocurrency's journey from a niche technology to a global phenomenon has led to varying levels of adoption and acceptance in different countries. In this section, we'll explore how cryptocurrencies are being embraced around the world and the factors that influence their reception.

Varying Levels of Adoption

Cryptocurrency adoption differs greatly from country to country. Some nations have embraced cryptocurrencies and blockchain technology, while others have taken a more cautious approach due to concerns about volatility, regulation, and potential risks.

Leading the Way: Cryptocurrency-Friendly Countries

Several countries have emerged as leaders in cryptocurrency adoption:

Switzerland: Known as "Crypto Valley," Switzerland has created a favorable environment for blockchain and cryptocurrency startups with its friendly regulations and business-friendly policies.

Singapore: Singapore has fostered a thriving cryptocurrency ecosystem through regulatory clarity and support for innovation.

Estonia: Estonia is exploring the use of blockchain technology in various sectors, including governance and healthcare.

Regulatory Challenges and Approaches

Cryptocurrency regulations vary widely, from outright bans to embracing innovation:

Japan: Japan recognized Bitcoin as a legal tender and has a well-regulated cryptocurrency exchange industry.

China: China has banned initial coin offerings (ICOs) and shut down cryptocurrency exchanges, although it continues to explore blockchain technology.

India: India has had a fluctuating relationship with cryptocurrencies, with the government considering both bans and regulations.

Economic and Social Factors

The level of cryptocurrency adoption often depends on a country's economic and social conditions:

Economic Uncertainty: Cryptocurrencies gain popularity in countries with economic instability or high inflation rates, as they offer an alternative store of value.

Remittances: Cryptocurrencies can provide a cheaper and faster method for cross-border remittances, making them appealing in countries where remittances play a significant role in the economy.

Public Awareness and Education

Cryptocurrency adoption is often linked to public awareness and education. Countries with higher levels of tech-savviness and digital literacy tend to have more individuals interested in and using cryptocurrencies.

Global Financial Powerhouses

Financial powerhouses like the United States and European Union countries are also grappling with cryptocurrency adoption. Regulatory frameworks and government policies play a crucial role in determining the level of acceptance and integration.

Bridging the Gap with Education

In countries where cryptocurrencies are less adopted, educational initiatives and awareness campaigns can play a vital role in introducing people to the concept and benefits of digital currencies.

Cryptocurrency Regulation and its Effects on the Economy

The growth of cryptocurrencies has prompted governments and regulatory bodies to grapple with how to manage this innovative technology within their existing frameworks. In this section, we'll delve into the complexities of cryptocurrency regulation and the ways it can impact economies.

Striking a Balance: Regulation and Innovation

Governments face the challenge of finding a balance between fostering innovation and protecting consumers and investors. Cryptocurrencies have introduced new opportunities and risks that require careful consideration.

Consumer Protection

Regulation aims to safeguard consumers from fraud, scams, and unfair practices. It also ensures that investors receive accurate information about cryptocurrencies before making investment decisions.

A Global Patchwork of Regulations

Cryptocurrency regulation varies widely from country to country. Some nations have embraced cryptocurrencies with friendly regulations, while others have taken a cautious approach due to concerns about money laundering, tax evasion, and market manipulation.

Regulatory Approaches

Regulatory approaches can be categorized into different strategies:

Proactive Regulation: Some countries, like Switzerland and Singapore, have chosen to proactively regulate the cryptocurrency space, offering legal clarity, and fostering innovation.

Restrictive Measures: Other countries, such as China, have taken restrictive measures like banning ICOs and shutting down cryptocurrency exchanges due to concerns about financial stability.

Wait-and-See Approach: Some countries are taking a wait-and-see approach, observing how the technology develops before implementing specific regulations.

Impact on Innovation

Cryptocurrency regulation can impact innovation by either providing a conducive environment for startups or stifling their growth. Friendly regulations can attract investment and talent to a country, while restrictive measures can drive innovation elsewhere.

Taxation and Reporting

Governments are exploring how to tax cryptocurrencies and ensure that individuals report their cryptocurrency-related income accurately. This is a complex issue, as cryptocurrencies can be difficult to track and value.

Effects on Investment and Business

Clear and supportive regulations can encourage investment in the cryptocurrency sector and the development of blockchain-based businesses. Conversely, unclear, or stringent regulations can hinder growth and investment.

Blockchain Beyond Cryptocurrencies

Regulation doesn't just impact cryptocurrencies; it also affects the broader adoption of blockchain technology. Many industries are exploring the use of blockchain for various applications beyond digital currencies.

International Coordination

As cryptocurrencies operate on a global scale, international coordination on regulations is essential to prevent regulatory arbitrage and ensure consistent treatment of cryptocurrencies.

Conclusion

Cryptocurrency regulation is a complex and evolving field that carries significant implications for economies around the world. Striking the right balance between innovation, consumer protection, and regulatory clarity is crucial for ensuring the responsible growth of the cryptocurrency industry. As governments continue to navigate this landscape, the effects of cryptocurrency regulation on economies will continue to unfold.

Large Bitcoin Holders ($1B+) August 2023

	Entity	Bitcoin	# of addresses	Address
Individuals	Satoshi Nakamoto	~1,100,000 BTC	~22,000	
	Unknown entity	94,643 BTC	1	bc1qazcm763858nkj2dj986etajv6wquslv8uxwczt
	Unknown entity	94,505 BTC	1	37XuVSEpWW4trkfmvWzegTHQt7BdktSKUs
	Winklevoss twins	~70,000 BTC	?	
	Unknown entity	69,370 BTC	1	bc1qa5wkgaew2dkv56kfvj49j0av5nml45x9ek9hz6
	Unknown entity	59,300 BTC	1	bc1qd4ysezhmypwty5dnw7c8nqy5h5nxg0xqsvaefd0qn5kq32vwnwqqgv4rzr
	Unknown entity	53,880 BTC	1	1LdRcdxfbSnmCYYNdeYpUnztiYzVfBEQeC
	Unknown entity	51,830 BTC	1	1AC4fMwgY8j9onSbXEWeH6Zan8QGM5dmtA
Exchanges	Binance	~498,147 BTC	4+	
	Bitfinex	~192,508 BTC	2+	
	OKEX	~118,334 BTC	8+	
	Robinhood	~118,300 BTC	1	bc1ql49ydapnjafl5t2cp9zqpjwe6pdgmxy98859v2
	MtGox hack 2011	79,957 BTC	1	1FeexV6bAHb8ybZjqQMjJrcCrHGW9sb6uF
Governments	US Department of Justice			
	(Bitfinex 2016 hack)	94,643 BTC	1	bc1qazcm763858nkj2dj986etajv6wquslv8uxwczt
	(Unknown source)	79,957 BTC	1	bc1qa5wkgaew2dkv56kfvj49j0av5nml45x9ek9hz6
Companies	Grayscale	~643,572 BTC	?	
	Block.one	~140,000 BTC	?	
	MicroStrategy	152,333 BTC	?	

Image Source: River financial (www.river.com)

CHAPTER 21 CRYPTOCURRENCY FOR EVERYDAY USE

Integrating Cryptocurrencies into Daily Transactions

Cryptocurrencies, once seen as a niche technology, are now gradually finding their way into our everyday lives as a viable form of payment. In this section, we'll explore how cryptocurrencies are being integrated into daily transactions, making them a convenient and accessible option for people around the world.

1. Digital Wallets and Mobile Apps

Just like you use apps on your smartphone for various tasks, you can also use mobile wallets to store and manage your cryptocurrencies. These digital wallets allow you to send and receive cryptocurrencies easily. You might have heard of wallets like Coinbase, Trust Wallet, or MetaMask.

2. Online and In-Person Payments

Cryptocurrencies are becoming increasingly accepted as a

means of payment. You can use them for online purchases, whether you're buying clothes, ordering food, or even booking flights and hotels. Some online retailers and service providers now offer the option to pay with cryptocurrencies.

3. Peer-to-Peer Transactions

Imagine you owe a friend some money for a movie ticket or a meal. Instead of using traditional cash, you can quickly send them cryptocurrency using your smartphone. Peer-to-peer transactions like these are becoming more common, especially for smaller payments.

4. International Transactions

Sending money internationally can be expensive and time-consuming through traditional banking channels. Cryptocurrencies, on the other hand, offer a fast and cost-effective way to send funds across borders. This is especially beneficial for people who have family or friends living in different countries.

5. Micropayments and Content Creation

Cryptocurrencies also enable micropayments, which are tiny amounts of money that can be sent online. This is particularly useful for content creators. For example, you could support your favorite YouTuber by sending them a small amount of cryptocurrency as a tip for their content.

6. Cryptocurrency Debit Cards

Some companies are creating debit cards that allow you to spend your cryptocurrencies just like you would spend traditional money. These cards convert your chosen cryptocurrency into the local currency at the time of purchase.

7. Challenges and Advantages

While cryptocurrencies offer convenience, they also come with challenges. The value of cryptocurrencies can be volatile, meaning their price can change rapidly. This can impact the amount you spend or receive in everyday transactions. Additionally, not all places accept cryptocurrencies yet, so you might need to convert them to traditional currency for certain purchases.

8. Security and Privacy

Using cryptocurrencies for everyday transactions requires attention to security. Make sure to use reputable wallets and follow best practices for keeping your private keys safe. While transactions are recorded on the blockchain and are transparent, your personal information is kept private.

Cryptocurrency Adoption in E-commerce and Retail

The world of e-commerce and retail is undergoing a significant transformation as cryptocurrencies are gradually making their mark as a legitimate form of payment. In this section, we'll delve into how cryptocurrencies are being adopted in the realm of online shopping and traditional retail environments.

1. Online Shopping with Cryptocurrencies

Online retailers are starting to embrace cryptocurrencies as a payment option. When you're shopping on the internet, you might notice a "Pay with Crypto" button alongside traditional payment methods like credit cards and PayPal. This allows you to use your cryptocurrencies to purchase everything from clothes and electronics to digital goods and services.

2. Decentralized Marketplaces

In addition to traditional online retailers, there are decentralized marketplaces that operate exclusively with cryptocurrencies. These platforms allow individuals to buy and sell goods and services directly, without intermediaries. This decentralized nature aligns with the core principles of cryptocurrencies.

3. Faster and Borderless Transactions: One of the advantages of using cryptocurrencies for e-commerce is the speed of transactions. Cryptocurrency payments can be processed quickly, which means you don't have to wait for banks to confirm the transaction. Additionally, since cryptocurrencies are not tied to specific countries, they facilitate borderless transactions without the

need for currency conversion.

4. Security and Fraud Prevention: Cryptocurrency transactions are secure and irreversible, which can help prevent fraud. Unlike credit card payments, which can be reversed through chargebacks, once a cryptocurrency transaction is confirmed on the blockchain, it cannot be altered.

5. Incentives and Rewards: Some e-commerce platforms offer incentives for customers who use cryptocurrencies for payment. These incentives might include discounts, cashback, or exclusive deals for cryptocurrency users.

6. Traditional Retail Adoption

Beyond the online world, cryptocurrencies are also making their way into traditional brick-and-mortar stores. Some retailers are installing point-of-sale (POS) systems that allow customers to pay with cryptocurrencies in physical stores. This blurs the lines between online and offline shopping experiences.

7. Challenges and Considerations

While cryptocurrency adoption in e-commerce and retail shows promise, there are challenges to overcome. One major challenge is the volatility of cryptocurrencies. The value of a cryptocurrency can change significantly in a short period, which might make it challenging for retailers to price their products accurately.

8. The Future of Shopping

As more retailers and platforms adopt cryptocurrencies, the future of shopping is likely to become more diverse and inclusive. Cryptocurrencies offer an alternative payment option that caters to individuals who prefer digital transactions and those who want to explore innovative financial solutions.

Conclusion

Cryptocurrency adoption in e-commerce and retail is gradually changing the way we shop and make payments. The convenience, speed, and security offered by cryptocurrencies are reshaping the online shopping experience and influencing how traditional retailers approach payments. While challenges like volatility persist, ongoing developments and increasing adoption by both retailers and consumers contribute to the growing integration of cryptocurrencies into the world of commerce.

CHAPTER 22 CRYPTO SCAMS AND HOW TO AVOID THEM

Identifying Common Crypto Scams

Cryptocurrency's growing popularity has unfortunately led to the rise of various scams and fraudulent schemes targeting unsuspecting individuals. In this section, we'll explore some of the most common crypto scams and how to recognize them.

1. Ponzi Schemes

Ponzi schemes promise high returns on investments, often relying on new investments to pay returns to earlier investors. These schemes eventually collapse when the influx of new funds slows down, leaving many investors with significant losses.

2. Fake Initial Coin Offerings (ICOs)

Scammers create fake ICOs, promising groundbreaking projects and huge returns to attract investors. After collecting funds, these fraudsters disappear, leaving investors with worthless tokens.

3. Phishing Attacks

Phishing attacks involve tricking individuals into revealing their private keys, passwords, or other sensitive information by impersonating legitimate entities through fake websites, emails, or social media accounts.

4. Fake Exchanges

Scammers set up fake cryptocurrency exchanges that appear legitimate. Users are enticed to deposit funds, only to find that they are unable to withdraw or access their cryptocurrencies.

5. Pump and Dump Schemes

In pump-and-dump schemes, scammers artificially inflate the price of a low-value cryptocurrency through false or exaggerated claims. Once the price rises, they sell their holdings, causing the price to crash and leaving other investors at a loss.

6. Social Media and Celebrity Impersonation

Scammers impersonate well-known figures or celebrities on social media, promoting fraudulent giveaways or investment opportunities that require individuals to send cryptocurrency to a specific address.

Tips to Protect Yourself from Fraudulent Schemes

As crypto space continues to grow, it's important to be vigilant and take precautions to safeguard your investments and personal information. Here are some tips to protect yourself from falling victim to crypto scams.

1. Research Thoroughly

Before investing in any project or cryptocurrency, conduct thorough research. Verify the team behind the project, read the whitepaper, and assess its legitimacy.

2. Be Skeptical of High Returns

If an investment promises unrealistically high returns with little to no risk, it's likely too good to be true. Avoid investments that sound too enticing and do not align with typical market trends.

3. Use Reputable Exchanges

When buying, selling, or trading cryptocurrencies, use well-known and reputable exchanges. Research the exchange's history, security measures, and user reviews before using their services.

4. Protect Your Private Keys

Never share your private keys, passwords, or sensitive information with anyone. Store your private keys securely offline and use hardware wallets for added protection.

5. Verify URLs and Websites

Always double-check the URL of a website before entering your login credentials or making transactions. Scammers often create fake websites that resemble legitimate ones to steal your information.

6. Educate Yourself

Stay informed about the latest scams and security measures in crypto space. Educating yourself about potential risks will empower you to make informed decisions and avoid falling for fraudulent schemes.

Conclusion

Crypto scams can be devastating, leading to financial losses and the compromise of personal information. By being aware of common scams, staying informed, and following best practices, you can significantly reduce your risk of falling victim to fraudulent schemes. Remember that in the world of cryptocurrencies, vigilance and caution are your best allies in navigating safely through the digital landscape.

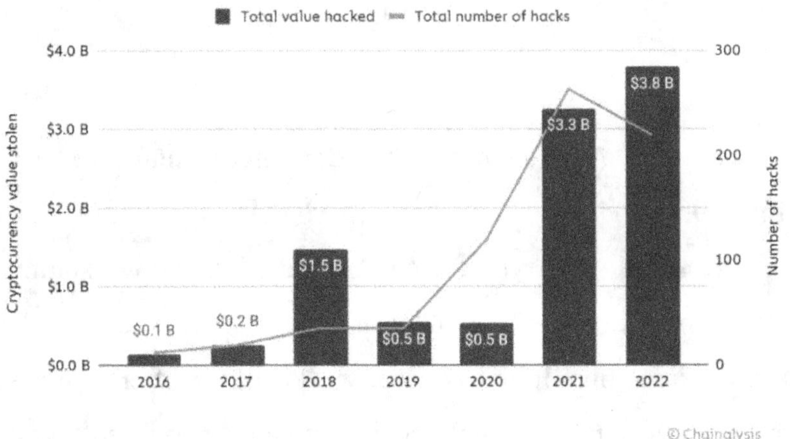

Image Source: Chainalysis (www.chainalysis.com)

CHAPTER 23 CRYPTOCURRENCY INVESTING: STRATEGIES AND TIPS

Investment Approaches for Beginners and Experienced Investors

Investing in cryptocurrencies can be both exciting and rewarding, but it's important to approach it with careful planning and consideration. In this section, we'll explore different investment approaches suitable for both beginners and experienced investors in the cryptocurrency space.

1. Long-Term vs. Short-Term

Long-Term: Long-term investing involves buying and holding cryptocurrencies with the expectation that their value will increase over time. This approach requires patience and a belief in the long-term potential of the chosen cryptocurrencies.

Short-Term: Short-term trading, often referred to as day trading, involves buying and selling cryptocurrencies within short timeframes to capitalize on price fluctuations. This approach requires a deep understanding of market trends and technical analysis.

2. Dollar-cost averaging (DCA)

DCA is a strategy where you invest a fixed amount of money at regular intervals, regardless of the cryptocurrency's price. This approach helps to mitigate the impact of price volatility and allows you to accumulate cryptocurrencies over time.

3. Fundamental Analysis

For those willing to do in-depth research, fundamental analysis involves evaluating the underlying factors that can impact the value of a cryptocurrency. This includes examining the project's technology, team, partnerships, and real-world use cases.

4. Technical Analysis

Technical analysis involves studying price charts and patterns to predict future price movements. This approach requires knowledge of chart indicators and patterns and is often used by short-term traders.

Diversification and Risk Management in Crypto Portfolios

As with any investment, diversification and risk management are crucial when building a cryptocurrency portfolio. Let's explore how these principles can help you navigate the volatile world of cryptocurrencies.

1. Diversification

Diversification involves spreading your investments across a variety of different cryptocurrencies rather than putting all your funds into one. This helps reduce the risk associated with the poor performance of a single cryptocurrency.

2. Risk Tolerance

Assess your risk tolerance before investing in cryptocurrencies. Cryptocurrencies can be highly volatile, and it's important to invest only what you can afford to lose without jeopardizing your financial stability.

3. Portfolio Rebalancing

Regularly review and rebalance your portfolio to ensure that your investments align with your goals and risk tolerance. If one cryptocurrency's value has grown significantly, it might be wise to sell a portion and redistribute the funds.

4. Stay Informed

Keep yourself updated with the latest news and developments in the cryptocurrency space. Market sentiment can be influenced by news, regulatory changes, technological advancements, and other factors.

5. Secure Storage

Ensure the security of your investments by using reputable

cryptocurrency wallets. Hardware wallets offer an extra layer of security by keeping your private keys offline.

6. Avoid FOMO (Fear of Missing Out)

Making investment decisions based solely on the fear of missing out can lead to impulsive choices and losses. Take the time to research and make informed decisions rather than succumbing to FOMO.

Conclusion

Cryptocurrency investing offers a range of approaches, from long-term strategies to short-term trading, and requires careful consideration of risk management and portfolio diversification. By understanding your investment goals, risk tolerance, and the principles of diversification, you can navigate the complex world of cryptocurrencies with greater confidence and make informed investment decisions.

Curve DAO (CRV) Token: Unveiling the Power of Decentralized Governance

Curve DAO is not just a cryptocurrency but the gateway to decentralized governance within the Curve Finance ecosystem. At its heart lies CRV, the native token that fuels this decentralized decision-making powerhouse. So, how does Curve DAO function, and what's the story behind its creation?

Empowering the CRV Token Holders

Curve DAO opens its doors to CRV token holders, offering them a chance to actively participate in the decentralized governance of Curve Finance. To get in the game, they lock their CRV tokens for various durations, thereby gaining valuable voting power within the system. As a bonus, participants receive veCRV (vote escrowed CRV) tokens in return, determined by the number of CRV tokens they lock and the duration they choose (ranging from one week to four years).

Voting power depends on the number of locked CRV tokens and the duration of their lockup. For example, locking 1,000 CRV tokens for one year earns you a voting power of 250 veCRV. As the escrowed tokens approach their lock expiry, the voting power gradually decreases.

Moreover, users with a voting power of 2,500 veCRV can step into the role of proposal pioneers. They can submit new proposals for consideration and voting by other DAO members. These proposals are open for discussion on the Curve DAO governance forum, where users collectively shape the direction of Curve Finance.

The Curve DAO also introduces a nifty feature called the vote locking boost. With this feature, users have the potential to increase their rewards by up to 2.5 times on the liquidity they provide. This acts as a compelling incentive for users to actively partake in Curve

Finance governance, as they reap a larger share of the daily CRV inflation.

A Glimpse into Curve Finance and CRV DAO Token's Past

Curve Finance, a decentralized exchange (DEX), came into existence in January 2020, focusing on enabling the seamless exchange of ERC-20 tokens for stablecoins. As the DeFi frenzy ignited in the latter half of 2020, Curve Finance found itself at the centre of explosive growth and decided to inaugurate the Curve DAO in August.

This novel financial project was initiated by Michael Egorov, a Russian scientist with a background in crypto projects. Egorov played a significant role in the founding of several prominent crypto ventures, including NuCypher and LoanCoin. He outlined his vision for Curve Finance in the StableSwap whitepaper in November 2019.

Some notable investors in Curve Finance include Coinbase Ventures, Digital Currency Group (DCG), Framework Ventures, and RR2Capital. The community grant program, introduced in October 2020, aimed to bolster the DeFi ecosystem on Curve's platform and in the broader market.

In November 2020, Curve Finance integrated Chainlink Price Feeds, a pivotal move to enhance security by eliminating exposure to flash loan attacks. This integration provided users with a reliable pricing mechanism for the LP tokens supported by the platform.

The Curve DAO and CRV token are key players in the world of

decentralized finance, giving users the power to shape the future of Curve Finance and be rewarded for their active involvement.

CHAPTER 24 PRIVACY AND ANONYMITY IN THE CRYPTOCURRENCY WORLD

Exploring Privacy-Centric Cryptocurrencies and Techniques

Privacy and anonymity are important aspects of the cryptocurrency world, as they allow users to keep their financial transactions and personal information confidential. In this section, we'll delve into the concept of privacy-centric cryptocurrencies and the techniques they use to protect users' identities.

1. The Importance of Privacy

Privacy is a fundamental right in the digital age, and it's no different when it comes to cryptocurrencies. Just like you wouldn't want strangers to know how much money you have or what you spend it on, privacy in the cryptocurrency world ensures that your financial information remains confidential.

2. Privacy-Centric Cryptocurrencies

Privacy-centric cryptocurrencies are designed specifically to enhance the privacy and anonymity of transactions. Examples of privacy-focused cryptocurrencies include Monero, Zcash, and Dash. These cryptocurrencies implement advanced cryptographic techniques to achieve privacy.

3. Ring Signatures and Confidential Transactions

One of the techniques used by privacy-centric cryptocurrencies is called ring signatures. This technique mixes the spender's transaction with multiple other transactions, making it challenging to determine which transaction corresponds to the actual spender.

Confidential transactions are another technique that conceals the transaction amount. While the transaction is verified by the network, the exact amount remains encrypted.

4. Stealth Addresses

Privacy-focused cryptocurrencies often use stealth addresses. When you receive funds, a unique address is generated for each transaction. This means that the sender can only see that you received funds, but they can't link that transaction to your identity or other transactions.

5. Challenges and Trade-Offs

While privacy-centric cryptocurrencies offer enhanced privacy, they also face challenges. For instance, some governments and regulatory bodies may express concerns about the potential for these cryptocurrencies to be used for illegal activities. Striking a balance between privacy and regulatory compliance is an ongoing challenge.

6. User Responsibility

Using privacy-centric cryptocurrencies requires a degree of responsibility from users. While these cryptocurrencies enhance privacy, practices like reusing addresses can compromise anonymity. Users need to educate themselves about best practices to maintain their privacy effectively.

7. Evolution of Privacy Techniques

The field of privacy and cryptography is ever evolving. Researchers and developers are continually working on new techniques to improve the privacy features of cryptocurrencies, ensuring that users can have more control over their financial information.

Balancing Privacy and Regulatory Compliance

The world of cryptocurrencies presents a unique challenge when it comes to privacy and regulatory compliance. In this section, we'll explore how the balance between user privacy and adhering to regulations is navigated in the cryptocurrency world.

1. The Regulatory Landscape

Governments and regulatory bodies have a responsibility to prevent illegal activities, such as money laundering and terrorism financing. To achieve this, they often require financial institutions, including cryptocurrency exchanges, to follow know-your-customer (KYC) and anti-money laundering (AML) regulations.

2. The Role of Anonymity

While cryptocurrencies offer increased privacy and anonymity, they can also be misused for illicit activities due to their pseudonymous nature. This has led to concerns among regulators and calls for enhanced transparency.

3. Privacy Coins and Regulation

Privacy-centric cryptocurrencies, also known as privacy coins, have faced scrutiny from regulators due to their potential use in illegal activities. Some exchanges have delisted certain privacy coins to comply with regulatory requirements and mitigate potential risks.

4. The Need for Solutions

Striking a balance between user privacy and regulatory compliance is a complex challenge. On the one hand, individuals value their privacy and the right to control their financial information. On the other hand, regulatory compliance is essential to prevent financial crimes and protect the broader financial system.

5. Regulatory Approaches

Different countries have taken various approaches to regulating cryptocurrencies. Some have embraced them with clear regulations that address both privacy concerns and regulatory compliance. Others have taken a cautious stance, imposing restrictions on privacy-centric cryptocurrencies.

6. Transparent Transactions

To address regulatory concerns while preserving user privacy, some cryptocurrency projects aim to combine transparency with privacy. They provide the option for transparent transactions, where users can choose to disclose transaction details for regulatory purposes while still having the option for private transactions.

7. Self-Regulation and Collaboration

Some segments of the cryptocurrency industry are working toward self-regulation. By establishing best practices and standards, the industry aims to demonstrate a commitment to responsible behavior and cooperation with regulators.

8. Education and Awareness

As the cryptocurrency space evolves, education and awareness play a crucial role. Users, investors, and industry players need to understand both the benefits of privacy in cryptocurrencies and the importance of adhering to regulatory requirements.

Conclusion

Balancing privacy and regulatory compliance is a challenge that requires thoughtful consideration and collaboration among users, developers, exchanges, and regulatory bodies. While privacy-centric cryptocurrencies provide valuable privacy options, it's essential to find ways to prevent misuse and protect the integrity of the financial system. As the cryptocurrency landscape continues to develop, finding common ground between privacy and regulation will be crucial for the sustainable growth of the industry.

CHAPTER 25 7 BEST RULES FOR CRYPTOCURRENCY INVESTMENT

1-The Rules of MP: "Make your financial future as stylish as your taste for luxury. When you want something cool, save up. Take half of the price and invest it to grow your money."

(In detail): The "Rules of Mp" is a guiding principle that advocates a prudent approach to personal finance and investment. It encourages individuals to align their desires for luxury items, such as cars, watches, or high-end clothing, with a responsible commitment to long-term financial security. According to this law, when one desires to acquire an expensive asset, one should simultaneously allocate 50% of the purchase price into various forms of investments.

This allocation is structured as follows: 50% of the desired purchase price should be directed into cryptocurrencies, reflecting the potential for high returns in the dynamic digital asset space. Another 30% should be invested in stocks, providing a diversified exposure to traditional financial markets. The remaining 20%

should be directed into a savings account, which serves as a secure reservoir for future needs and emergencies.

By adhering to the "rule of Mp," individuals aim to strike a balance between enjoying the present and securing their financial well-being for the future. It underscores the importance of responsible spending and investment, ensuring that while one enjoys the pleasures of life, one also builds a substantial financial cushion for the long term. This law encourages a holistic approach to personal finance, promoting financial growth and stability alongside the pursuit of personal desires.

2-The Rule of P: "Plunge into the vast digital ocean, ride the information waves, and moor your investments in top 20 cryptos. When you reach the shores of profit, let the currents of tomorrow carry you to new adventures."

(In detail): The "Rule of P" is a doctrine founded on thorough research and a commitment to securing your financial future in the world of cryptocurrencies. It emphasizes comprehensive knowledge and a thoughtful investment strategy.

This principle encourages individuals to delve into the wealth of information available on cryptocurrencies, focusing on well-established, top-tier coins within the market's top 20. By conducting comprehensive research, you can gain a deeper understanding of these digital assets, forming a solid foundation for your investment choices.

The core of the "Rule of P" is to invest in reputable and

established cryptocurrencies, recognized for their stability and long-term potential. By allocating a significant portion of your portfolio to these top-performing coins, you aim to construct a reliable and secure financial base.

As profits accumulate over time, this law advises dedicating a portion of these gains to explore future options. These future options might include new investment opportunities, further education, or personal ventures. The objective is to leverage the consistent income generated from your investments to explore new possibilities and seize opportunities as they arise. Specifically, it recommends allocating 50% of the profits earned from these investments to finance these future endeavours.

The "Rule of P" champions a patient and well-informed approach to cryptocurrency investment, highlighting the significance of research, security, and the use of profits to facilitate future financial growth and flexibility. It strikes a balance between establishing a secure financial foundation and creating prospects for future expansion.

3-Rule of D: "Follow the crowd, copy the experts, and secure your gains. Stick to 20% or 10% stop loss in leveraged trades. That's the ticket to a winning game."

(In detail): The "Rule of D" is a guideline rooted in the practice of copy trading and the disciplined approach of securing profits in leveraged investments. It emphasizes prudent risk management and learning from the expertise of others.

This rule encourages individuals to embrace the concept of copy trading, a strategy where you follow the investment decisions of experienced traders or experts in the field. By doing so, you can leverage their knowledge and experience to make informed investment choices.

The core of the "Rule of D" is to prioritize risk management. In leveraged trades, it suggests implementing a stop-loss strategy. Specifically, it advises using a 20% or 10% stop loss, which means that if the trade goes against you, you'll limit your losses by exiting the trade when your investment has declined by the specified percentage.

This rule reinforces the idea that consistent, smaller profits and effective risk management can lead to long-term success. By following the guidance of experienced traders, you can increase your chances of making informed investment decisions and minimizing potential losses.

The "Rule of D" advocates a disciplined approach to trading and emphasizes the importance of balancing the desire for profits with prudent risk management. It serves as a roadmap for those seeking a winning strategy in the world of leveraged investments.

4-Rule of M: "Invest with care, using only 30-45% of what's left after taxes and bills. Keep the rest safe and sound."

(In detail): The "Rule of M" is a financial guideline rooted in the principles of responsible and sustainable cryptocurrency investing. It underscores the importance of understanding your financial capacity and allocating a portion of your resources prudently.

This rule advises individuals to approach cryptocurrency investments with diligence. Specifically, it suggests that investors use only 30-45% of the funds that remain after they've covered essential financial commitments, including taxes and necessary bills. The remaining portion should be kept in a safe and easily accessible financial instrument, ensuring financial stability and security.

The "Rule of M" serves as a reminder of the significance of maintaining a balanced and well-considered approach to cryptocurrency investments. By adhering to this rule, individuals can enjoy the potential benefits of cryptocurrency investments while safeguarding their overall financial well-being. It emphasizes the importance of not overextending into risky investments and maintaining a financial cushion for unexpected expenses and emergencies.

5-Rule of N: "If life's good as it is, why rock the boat? Not investing in crypto is a saving strategy too, just like not playing the betting game."

(In detail): The "Rule N" advocates for a flexible and balanced approach to cryptocurrency investment. It acknowledges that if an individual is content with their current financial situation and lifestyle, refraining from investing in cryptocurrency can be a sound financial decision.

This rule highlights the importance of understanding that not investing in cryptocurrency is a legitimate and responsible choice. It aligns with the notion that if you're comfortable with your current financial state, there's no need to venture into the world of cryptocurrencies. Just as saving money is a valuable financial strategy, so is avoiding speculative investments in the cryptocurrency market.

"Rule N" encourages individuals to make choices that best suit their financial goals and risk tolerance. It recognizes that there are various paths to financial security.

and not all of them involve cryptocurrency investments. It underlines the significance of aligning your financial decisions with your personal comfort and objectives, whether that includes saving money through traditional means or engaging in cryptocurrency investments.

6 -Rule of V: "Find your financial flow and embrace the freedom to choose. If cryptocurrencies align with your rhythm, go ahead; if not, take comfort in the knowledge that you're safeguarding your finances and making mindful decisions."

(In detail): The "Rule of V" signifies a balanced approach to investment, prioritizing individual preferences and financial circumstances. It harmonizes the principles of financial autonomy and responsible allocation of resources without specifying particular rules.

This rule encourages individuals to align their investment decisions with their unique financial rhythms. It acknowledges that cryptocurrency investments may not be suitable for everyone, and that's acceptable. If cryptocurrency aligns with your financial goals and risk tolerance, feel free to explore this option. If it doesn't, you can take confidence in the fact that responsible saving and prudently managing your financial resources are solid financial strategies.

The "Rule of V" underscores the importance of choice and flexibility in financial decision-making. It recognizes that individuals have diverse financial aspirations and varying comfort levels with risk. Whether you choose to invest in cryptocurrency, save conservatively, or opt for a blend of financial strategies, the critical element is to follow your unique path and remain attuned to your financial circumstances and objectives.

7 -Rule of F: "Stay frosty, my friends. When market news gets your heart racing, take a breath. Check before you wreck; false alarms might make you buy high and sell low."

(In detail): The "Rule F" is a guiding principle that encourages a prudent response to market news in the cryptocurrency space, considering the potential impact of FUD (Fear, Uncertainty, Doubt) and FOMO (Fear of Missing Out) on investment decisions.

This rule emphasizes the importance of maintaining a calm and rational approach when confronted with market news that can trigger emotional responses. It advises individuals not to immediately react to sensational or unverified news without checking the credibility of the sources. Blindly following the crowd based on unsubstantiated information can lead to unfavourable outcomes, such as buying high and selling low.

"Rule F" serves as a reminder to prioritize fact-checking and critical thinking over impulsive reactions to market news. By doing so, individuals can make more informed investment decisions and mitigate the potential negative impact of FUD and FOMO on their portfolios. It advocates a patient and research-driven approach to handling market information, ultimately leading to more prudent financial choices.

CRYPTOCURRENCY SLANG WORDS AND PHRASES

HODL: Originally a typo for "hold," it now stands for "Hold on for Dear Life." It means to keep your cryptocurrency investments, regardless of market fluctuations.

FUD: "Fear, Uncertainty, Doubt." FUD is often spread to create fear and panic in the market, leading to price drops.

FOMO: "Fear of Missing Out." It describes the anxiety of missing out on potential profits, which can lead to impulsive buying.

SAFU: "Secure Asset Fund for Users." Binance created this fund to compensate users in case of a security breach or hack.

ATH: "All-Time High." It signifies the highest price ever reached by a cryptocurrency.

ALT: Short for "altcoin," any cryptocurrency other than Bitcoin is considered an "alt."

DUMP: A sharp and sudden decline in the price of a cryptocurrency.

PUMP: A rapid increase in the price of a cryptocurrency.

BAGHOLDER: Someone who's stuck holding a depreciating cryptocurrency.

REKT: A humorous variation of "wrecked," meaning significant losses or a bad trade.

MOON: Refers to the expectation that a cryptocurrency's price will soar to astronomical levels.

BEAR MARKET: A prolonged period of declining prices in the cryptocurrency market.

BULL MARKET: A period of rising prices and optimism in the cryptocurrency market.

WHALE: An individual or entity that holds a large amount of cryptocurrency.

P2P: "Peer-to-Peer." Refers to a decentralized network where users interact directly without intermediaries.

DYOR: "Do Your Own Research." Encourages individuals to thoroughly research an investment before deciding.

ICO: "Initial Coin Offering." It's a way for new projects to raise funds by selling tokens to investors.

AIRDROP: Distributing free tokens to holders of a specific cryptocurrency.

DApp: "Decentralized Application." These are applications that run on blockchain networks and are not controlled by a single entity.

PAPER WALLET: A physical document containing public and private keys used for storing cryptocurrency offline.

REVERSAL: A change in the direction of a price trend, often signalling the end of a current trend.

FORK: A split in the blockchain, creating two separate chains with different rules, which can result in the birth of a new cryptocurrency.

LIQUIDITY: The ease with which an asset can be bought or sold without significantly affecting its price.

FUNDAMENTALS: The underlying characteristics and value of a cryptocurrency, such as its technology, use cases, and team.

STABLECOIN: A type of cryptocurrency designed to have a stable value, often pegged to a traditional currency like the US dollar.

FLOP: A term used to describe a project or cryptocurrency that fails to gain popularity or value.

WHITEPAPER: A detailed document describing the technology, purpose, and plans of a cryptocurrency project.

DELEGATED PROOF OF STAKE (DPoS): A consensus mechanism where a select group of individuals or entities is chosen to validate transactions and create new blocks.

SMART CONTRACT: Self-executing contracts with the terms of the agreement directly written into code.

MOONING: Refers to a cryptocurrency's price rapidly increasing to the point where it appears to be heading to the moon.

SATS/SATOSHIS: The smallest unit of Bitcoin, equivalent to 0.00000001 BTC.

WHITELIST: A list of approved participants in an initial coin offering (ICO) or token sale.

FOMOING: The act of buying a cryptocurrency due to fear of missing out (FOMO) on potential gains.

MARKET CAP: The total value of a cryptocurrency is calculated by multiplying its price by the total supply of coins.

LAMBO: Short for Lamborghini, often used humorously to represent extravagant purchases people might make with cryptocurrency gains.

PUMP AND DUMP: A scheme where the price of a cryptocurrency is artificially inflated (pumped) to attract investors, followed by a quick sell-off (dump).

WYCKOFF: A trading strategy and methodology developed by Richard Wyckoff for analysing and understanding market trends.

MAXI: Short for "maximalist," it describes someone who strongly believes in one specific cryptocurrency, often Bitcoin, to the exclusion of all others.

ALT SEASON: A period in which altcoins (cryptocurrencies other than Bitcoin) experience a significant increase in value.

FLIP/FLIPPENING: When one cryptocurrency overtakes another in market capitalization, it's referred to as a flip or flippening.

FLOOR: The lowest price point at which a cryptocurrency is expected to remain, providing a sense of support in a declining market.

SALT: This term is used to describe the act of lending cryptocurrency to earn interest.

BUIDL: A humorous twist on "HODL," emphasizing the importance of building and developing blockchain projects.

FAUCET: A website or app that gives away small amounts of cryptocurrency for free.

TX: Short for "transaction," it's commonly used in reference to the movement of cryptocurrency from one wallet to another.

DEX: "Decentralized Exchange." These platforms allow users to trade cryptocurrencies without a centralized intermediary.

MAX SUPPLY: The maximum number of coins that will ever be created for a particular cryptocurrency.

SWING TRADING: A trading strategy that involves making short to medium-term trades to capture price swings.

STAKING: The process of holding and locking up cryptocurrency in a wallet to support the operations of a blockchain network and earn rewards.

ONCHAIN: Refers to activities and data that occur directly on a blockchain, such as transactions and smart contract executions.

OFFCHAIN: Transactions and activities that happen outside the blockchain, often used in scaling solutions like the Lightning Network for Bitcoin.

SHILLING: The act of aggressively promoting a cryptocurrency or project for personal gain.

NONCE: A number used only once in cryptographic processes, often related to proof-of-work mining.

GAS: The fee required to process a transaction on a blockchain, often used in Ethereum.

SIGWIT: "Segregated Witness." A technology upgrade in Bitcoin that separates transaction data from witness data to improve scalability.

TOKEN: A digital asset issued on a blockchain that represents ownership or access to a specific utility.

APY: "Annual Percentage Yield." It represents the annualized return on an investment, often used in DeFi platforms.

ATOMIC SWAP: A technology that allows for the peer-to-peer exchange of one cryptocurrency for another without the need for a centralized intermediary.

REBASE: A mechanism used in some cryptocurrency projects to adjust the total supply of tokens based on market conditions.

DUSTING ATTACK: A strategy where small amounts of cryptocurrency are sent to numerous addresses, often to trace or spam users.

ORPHAN BLOCK: A block that is valid but not included in the main blockchain due to a competing block being added first.

YOLO: "You Only Live Once." A term used humorously to describe impulsive and high-risk cryptocurrency investments or trades.

REFERENCES

"In crafting this book on cryptocurrency, I have drawn inspiration from various sources, including websites, blogs, and expert opinions. These insights have enriched the content and perspectives presented herein. I am deeply appreciative of the valuable contributions made by these sources, as they have contributed significantly to the depth and breadth of the information shared. To ensure the integrity of this work and acknowledge the intellectual property of others, I have diligently referenced and cited specific sources throughout the book. Proper attribution is not only a mark of respect for the original authors but also a commitment to transparency and the responsible use of their ideas."

For this book, we harnessed artificial intelligence and OpenAI. If you spot any content or reference errors, contact us at info.cryptvel@gmail.com

- What Is Cryptocurrency? – Forbes Advisor: This article explains what cryptocurrency is, how it works, and what are its advantages and disadvantages.

https://www.forbes.com/advisor/investing/what-is-cryptocurrency/

- What Is Cryptography? - Investopedia: This article provides an overview of cryptography, its history, its types, and its applications.

https://www.investopedia.com/terms/c/cryptography.asp

- What Is Decentralization? - CoinDesk: This article describes the concept and importance of decentralization for cryptocurrencies and blockchain technology.

- https://www.coindesk.com/learn

- What is Blockchain Technology? - IBM Blockchain | IBM

- Blockchain - Wikipedia

- What Is Crypto Mining, and How Does It Work? - How-To Geek

- NiceHash - Leading Cryptocurrency Platform for Mining

- What is Cryptocurrency Mining? | How Bitcoin Mining Works - Webopedia

- https://www.techopedia.com

- Centralized vs Decentralized Exchanges | Alexandria

- Centralized vs Decentralized Exchanges | FLOLiO

- Centralized vs decentralized exchanges: The Ultimate Guide - HedgeBlog

- **coinmarketcap.com**
- **coindesk.com**
- **flolio.com**
- **blog.hedgehog.app**
- **fxempire.com**
- Altcoin Explained: Pros and Cons, Types, and Future - Investopedia
- 10 Best Altcoins Of July 2023 – Forbes Advisor
- Buterin, V. (2013). "Ethereum White Paper: A Next-Generation Smart Contract and Decentralized Application Platform."
- Tapscott, D., & Tapscott, A. (2016). "Blockchain Revolution: How the Technology Behind Bitcoin Is Changing Money, Business, and the World." Penguin.
- Antonopoulos, A. M. (2018). "Mastering Ethereum: Building Smart Contracts and DApps." O'Reilly Media.
- Wood, G. (2014). "Ethereum: A Secure Decentralized Generalised Transaction Ledger." Ethereum Project Yellow Paper.
- Narayanan, A., Bonneau, J., Felten, E., Miller, A., & Goldfeder, S. (2016). "Bitcoin and Cryptocurrency Technologies: A Comprehensive Introduction." Princeton University Press.
- Mougayar, W. (2016). "The Business Blockchain: Promise, Practice, and Application of the Next Internet Technology." Wiley.
- Ethereum Foundation. (2022). "Ethereum 2.0."
- Binance Blog. (2022). "BNB: Bridging the Crypto and Traditional Finance Worlds."

- Binance Academy. (2022).

- Buterin, V. (2014). A Next-Generation Smart Contract and Decentralized Application Platform. Ethereum White Paper.

- Wood, G. (2014). Ethereum: A Secure Decentralised Generalised Transaction Ledger. Ethereum Yellow Paper.

- Catalini, C., & Gans, J. S. (2020). Some Simple Economics of the Blockchain. NBER Working Paper Series.

- Narula, N., & Choi, J. (2020). Decentralized Finance: Overview and Opportunities for Financial Inclusion. MIT Connection Science Research Brief.

- Mougayar, W. (2021). The Basics of Bitcoins and Blockchains. New York: O'Reilly Media.

- Ali, R., Barrdear, J., Clews, R., & Southgate, J. (2014). Innovations in payment technologies and the emergence of digital currencies. Bank of England Quarterly Bulletin.

- Hayase, K. (2020). DeFi and Credit on Blockchains: A Value Layer for the Decentralized Finance Stack. arXiv preprint arXiv:2010.07763.

- Hoskinson, C., & Wood, G. (2017). Ethereum: A secure decentralised generalised transaction ledger. Ethereum Yellow Paper.

- Akinola, G., Enahoro, C., & Olatunji, M. O. (2021). The rise of decentralized finance (DeFi): Opportunities, challenges, and future directions. International Journal of Advanced Science and Technology, 30(3), 3679-3686.

- Hileman, G., & Rauchs, M. (2017). Global cryptocurrency

benchmarking study. Cambridge Centre for Alternative Finance.

- Narula, N., & Choi, J. (2020). Decentralized Finance: Overview and Opportunities for Financial Inclusion. MIT Connection Science Research Brief.

- World Bank Group. (2020). Global Findex Database 2017: Measuring Financial Inclusion and the Fintech Revolution.

- ConsenSys. (2020). DeFi in Emerging Markets: Understanding the Landscape and Unlocking Opportunities.

- Dusheyko, M., Kandyba, V., & Sholom, V. (2020). The State of DeFi. ConsenSys.

- Loonie, C. (2022). "Bull Market vs Bear Market: What's the Difference?" Investopedia. Retrieved from: https://www.investopedia.com/ask/answers/122314/what-difference-between-bull-market-and-bear-market.asp

- Chong, S. (2021). "Cryptocurrency Trends: Bull and Bear Markets." Cryptocurrency Facts. Retrieved from: https://cryptocurrencyfacts.com/bull-and-bear-markets/

- Mian, R. S. (2021). "How to Read Trends in Crypto." Investopedia. Retrieved from: https://www.investopedia.com/tech/how-to-read-trends-crypto/

- Cuthbertson, A. (2022). "Cryptocurrency Trading for Beginners: How to Read Price Charts." The Independent. Retrieved from: https://www.independent.co.uk/news/business/how-to-read-crypto-price-charts-b1991658.html

- Vanier, L. (2020). "Crypto Trading Strategies." Binance Academy. Retrieved from:

https://academy.binance.com/en/articles/crypto-trading-strategies

- Hussain, I., & Raza, S. (2021). "An Analysis of Cryptocurrency Market Trends and Strategies for Investment." Journal of Internet Banking and Commerce, 26(1), 1-12. Retrieved from: https://search.proquest.com/docview/2479562727

- Schneier, B. (2015). "Applied Cryptography: Protocols, Algorithms, and Source Code in C." John Wiley & Sons.

- Delfs, H., & Knebl, H. (2014). "Introduction to Cryptography: Principles and Applications." Springer.

- Bitcoin.org. (2021). "Bitcoin Whitepaper." Retrieved from: https://bitcoin.org/bitcoin.pdf

- Ethereum.org. (2021). "Ethereum Whitepaper." Retrieved from: https://ethereum.org/en/whitepaper/

- Pilkington, M. (2021). "Energy Consumption of Blockchain-Based Non-Fungible Tokens." Joule, 5(12), 2883-2885.

- Mims, C. (2021). "An NFT 'Unicorn'? Buzzy Video-Poker App Raises $80 Million in Funding." The Wall Street Journal.

- Chasan, E. (2022). "NFTs and the Copyright Debate." Reuters

- Alibhai, R. (2021). "Are NFTs a Bubble? Inside the Most Expensive NFT Sales Ever." BBC News.

- Kell, J. (2021). "NFTs Are Booming. So Is the Crypto Art Market's Fraud Problem." The New York Times.

- Newton, C. (2021). "The High-Flying World of NFT Art." The New York Times.

- Smith, L. (2021). "From Meme to Millions: The Nyan Cat NFT Saga." CNET.

- Ives, N. (2021). "NFTs: The Next Big Thing in Collectibles?" BBC News.

- Gopinath, P. (2022). "Blockchain-based Charitable Giving." Journal of Emerging Technologies in Accounting, 19(1), 25-36.

- Sisario, B. (2021). "Blockchain Is NFT-izing the Music Industry." The New York Times.

- Schneider, A. (2021). "The Impact of NFTs on Gaming and Virtual Real Estate." Cointelegraph.

- Chotiner, I. (2021). "Exploring NFTs Beyond the Art World: Music, Sports, and Beyond." Rolling Stone.

- Wallace, T. (2021). "NFTs and the Real Estate Industry: Fractional Ownership and Digital Land." Inman.

- Inversini, A., Longo, L., Sicilia, M. A., & Steels, L. (2022). "NFT and Digital Art: New Avenues of Interaction with Art." Digital Creativity, 1-16.

- Buterin, V. (2014). "A Next-Generation Smart Contract and Decentralized Application Platform." Ethereum White Paper.

- Cuthbertson, A. (2021). "NFTs: What Are They and Why Do They Matter?" The Independent.

- IBM Blockchain. (2021). "Non-Fungible Tokens: What Are They and Why Do They Matter?" IBM.

- Salzman, J., Chen, A., & Buckley, A. (2021). "The rise of NFTs and intellectual property issues: Challenges and solutions." Hogan Lovells.

- Nakamoto, S. (2008). "Bitcoin: A Peer-to-Peer Electronic Cash System." Bitcoin.org.

- Buterin, V., & Griffith, V. (2017). "Casper the Friendly Finality Gadget." Ethereum Foundation.

- Miers, I., Garman, C., Green, M., & Rubin, A. (2013). "Zerocoin: Anonymous Distributed E-Cash from Bitcoin." IEEE Symposium on Security and Privacy.

- Buterin, V. (2017). "A Proof of Stake Design Philosophy." Ethereum Wiki.

- Zamfir, V. (2019). "Introducing Casper the Friendly Finality Gadget." Ethereum Foundation.

- Bitcoin Energy Consumption Index. (n.d.). Digiconomist.

- Khurana, S., & Gupta, K. (2021). "Towards Proof of Useful Work for Blockchain: A Systematic Literature Review." Sustainable Computing: Informatics and Systems, 30, 100594.

- Wood, G. (2013). "Ethereum: A Secure Decentralized Generalized Transaction Ledger." Ethereum Project Yellow Paper.

- Eth2 Launch Pad. (n.d.). Ethereum Foundation.

- Buterin, V. (2017). "A Proof of Stake Design Philosophy." Ethereum Wiki.

- Bahga, A., & Madisetti, V. (2020). "Blockchain for Business." Cham, Switzerland: Springer Nature Switzerland AG.

- Novak, T., & Stanczyk, P. (2019). "Proof of Work Vs. Proof of Stake Consensus Mechanism: A Comparative Review." Security and Communication Networks, 2019, 1-12.

- Bano, S., Sonnino, A., Al-Bassam, M., Azouvi, S.,

McCorry, P., Meiklejohn, S., & Danezis, G. (2017). "SoK: Consensus in the Age of Blockchains." Proceedings of the 2017 IEEE Symposium on Security and Privacy.

- Atzei, N., Bartoletti, M., & Cimoli, T. (2017). "A survey of attacks on Ethereum smart contracts." arXiv preprint arXiv:1708.05630.

- García-Bañuelos, L., Cornejo, M. D. R., & de la Rosa, J. L. (2020). "Blockchain and Artificial Intelligence Integration: A Systematic Review." Electronics, 9(2), 186.

- Osterwalder, A., Pigneur, Y., Bernarda, G., & Smith, A. (2014). "Value Proposition Design: How to Create Products and Services Customers Want." John Wiley & Sons.

- Crosby, M., Pattanayak, P., Verma, S., & Kalyanaraman, V. (2016). "Blockchain technology: Beyond bitcoin." Applied Innovation, 2(6-10), 71-81.

- Swan, M. (2015). "Blockchain: blueprint for a new economy." O'Reilly Media, Inc.

- Clack, C., Bakshi, V., & Braine, L. (2016). "Smart Contract Templates: foundations, design landscape, and research directions." arXiv preprint arXiv:1608.00771.

- Tapscott, D., & Tapscott, A. (2016). "Blockchain revolution: how the technology behind bitcoin is changing money, business, and the world." Penguin.

- Szabo, N. (1997). "Formalizing and Securing Relationships on Public Networks." First Monday, 2(9).

- Buterin, V. (2014). "Ethereum White Paper: A Next-

Generation Smart Contract and Decentralized Application Platform." Ethereum Foundation.

- Sams, E. (2018). "Stablecoins: designing a price-stable cryptocurrency." O'Reilly Media, Inc.

- Mougayar, W. (2016). "The Business Blockchain: Promise, Practice, and Application of the Next Internet Technology." John Wiley & Sons.

- Monegro, J. (2019). "Fat Protocols." Placeholder.

- Raval, S. (2016). "Decentralized Applications: Harnessing Bitcoin's Blockchain Technology." O'Reilly Media, Inc.

- Clark, D., & Glen, C. (2019). "The Basics of Bitcoins and Blockchains." Page Street Publishing.

- Narula, N., & Yermack, D. (2018). "Bitcoin as Decentralized Money: Prices, Mining, and Network Security." National Bureau of Economic Research.

- Buterin, V. (2014). "A next-generation smart contract and decentralized application platform." Ethereum white paper.

- Mougayar, W. (2016). "The Business Blockchain: Promise, Practice, and Application of the Next Internet Technology." John Wiley & Sons.

- Clark, D., & Glen, C. (2019). "The Basics of Bitcoins and Blockchains." Page Street Publishing.

- Monegro, J. (2019). "Fat Protocols." Placeholder.

- Tapscott, D., & Tapscott, A. (2016). "Blockchain revolution: how the technology behind bitcoin is changing money, business, and the world." Penguin.

REFERENCES

- Swan, M. (2015). "Blockchain: blueprint for a new economy." O'Reilly Media, Inc.

- Antonopoulos, A. M. (2018). "Mastering Bitcoin: Unlocking Digital Cryptocurrencies." O'Reilly Media, Inc.

- Tapscott, D., & Tapscott, A. (2016). "Blockchain revolution: how the technology behind bitcoin is changing money, business, and the world." Penguin.

- Burniske, C., & Tatar, J. (2018). "Cryptoassets: The Innovative Investor's Guide to Bitcoin and Beyond." McGraw-Hill Education.

- Zohar, A. (2015). "Bitcoin: Under the Hood." Communications of the ACM.

- Buterin, V. (2014). "A next-generation smart contract and decentralized application platform." Ethereum white paper.

- Tapscott, D., & Tapscott, A. (2016). "Blockchain revolution: how the technology behind bitcoin is changing money, business, and the world." Penguin.

- Burniske, C., & Tatar, J. (2018). "Cryptoassets: The Innovative Investor's Guide to Bitcoin and Beyond." McGraw-Hill Education.

- Mougayar, W. (2016). "The Business Blockchain: Promise, Practice, and Application of the Next Internet Technology." John Wiley & Sons.

- Casey, M. J., & Vigna, P. (2018). "The Truth Machine: The Blockchain and the Future of Everything." St. Martin's Press.

- Antonopoulos, A. M. (2018). "Mastering Bitcoin: Unlocking

Digital Cryptocurrencies." O'Reilly Media, Inc.

- Casey, M. J., & Vigna, P. (2018). "The Truth Machine: The Blockchain and the Future of Everything." St. Martin's Press.

- Mougayar, W. (2016). "The Business Blockchain: Promise, Practice, and Application of the Next Internet Technology." John Wiley & Sons.

- Tapscott, D., & Tapscott, A. (2016). "Blockchain revolution: how the technology behind bitcoin is changing money, business, and the world." Penguin.

- Narayanan, A., Bonneau, J., Felten, E., Miller, A., & Goldfeder, S. (2016). "Bitcoin and Cryptocurrency Technologies: A Comprehensive Introduction." Princeton University Press.

- : DeFi Pulse. (2021). Total Value Locked (USD) in DeFi. Retrieved from [DeFi Pulse].

- : Axie Infinity. (2021). Axie Infinity: A digital nation. Retrieved from [Axie Infinity].

- : Decentraland. (2021). Decentraland: Create, explore and trade in the first-ever virtual world owned by its users. Retrieved from [Decentraland].

- : The Sandbox. (2021). The Sandbox: A decentralized gaming platform owned by players. Retrieved from [The Sandbox].

- : Enjin. (2021). Enjin: Blockchain game development platform. Retrieved from [Enjin].

- : University of Cambridge. (2021). Cambridge Bitcoin Electricity Consumption Index (CBECI). Retrieved from [CBECI].

- : Monetary Authority of Singapore. (2020). Payment

REFERENCES

Services Act 2019. Retrieved from [Payment Services Act 2019].

- : Swiss Federal Council. (2018). Federal Act on Financial Services (FinSA). Retrieved from [FinSA].

- : Malta Financial Services Authority. (2018). Virtual Financial Assets Act 2018. Retrieved from [Virtual Financial Assets Act 2018].

- Casey, M. J., & Vigna, P. (2018). "The Truth Machine: The Blockchain and the Future of Everything." St. Martin's Press.

- Tapscott, D., & Tapscott, A. (2016). "Blockchain revolution: how the technology behind Bitcoin is changing money, business, and the world." Penguin.

- Mougayar, W. (2016). "The Business Blockchain: Promise, Practice, and Application of the Next Internet Technology." John Wiley & Sons.

- Tapscott, D., & Tapscott, A. (2016). "Blockchain revolution: how the technology behind bitcoin is changing money, business, and the world." Penguin.

- Tapscott, D., & Tapscott, A. (2016). "Blockchain revolution: how the technology behind bitcoin is changing money, business, and the world." Penguin.

- Casey, M. J., & Vigna, P. (2018). "The Truth Machine: The Blockchain and the Future of Everything." St. Martin's Press.

- Casey, M. J., & Vigna, P. (2018). "The Truth Machine: The Blockchain and the Future of Everything." St. Martin's Press.

- Mougayar, W. (2016). "The Business Blockchain: Promise, Practice, and Application of the Next Internet Technology." John

Wiley & Sons.

- Vigna, P., & Casey, M. J. (2018). "The Truth Machine: The Blockchain and the Future of Everything." St. Martin's Press.

- Potts, J., & Barratt, T. (2016). "Cryptocurrencies as distributed community experiments." Springer.

- FTC Consumer Information. (n.d.). "Cryptocurrency Scams." Federal Trade Commission. Retrieved from https://www.consumer.ftc.gov/articles/cryptocurrency-scams

- Casey, M. J., & Vigna, P. (2018). "The Truth Machine: The Blockchain and the Future of Everything." St. Martin's Press.

- Mougayar, W. (2016). "The Business Blockchain: Promise, Practice, and Application of the Next Internet Technology." John Wiley & Sons.

- Narayanan, A., Bonneau, J., Felten, E., Miller, A., & Goldfeder, S. (2016). "Bitcoin and Cryptocurrency Technologies: A Comprehensive Introduction." Princeton University Press.

- Ruffing, T., Moreno-Sanchez, P., Kate, A., & Micali, S. (2014). "CoinShuffle: Practical Decentralized Coin Mixing for Bitcoin." Proceedings of the IEEE Symposium on Security and Privacy.

- Zohar, A. (2015). "Bitcoin: Under the Hood." Communications of the ACM.

- Yermack, D. (2015). "Is Bitcoin a real currency? An economic appraisal." In Handbook of Digital Currency (pp. 31-43). Elsevier.

- Greenberg, A. (2019). "The Internet's Horrifying New Trick to Rip Off Creators." Wired. Retrieved from https://www.wired.com/story/the-internets-horrifying-new-trick-to-rip-off-creators/

- Financial Action Task Force (FATF). (n.d.). "Virtual Assets Red Flag Indicators of Money Laundering and Terrorist Financing." Retrieved from https://www.fatf-gafi.org/publications/fatfrecommendations/documents/virtual-assets-red-flag-indicators.html

FINAL WORDS

As we reach the end of this journey through the fascinating world of cryptocurrency, it's essential to remember that the crypto landscape is continually evolving. The information presented in this book is accurate and up to date as of its publication. However, the crypto market is highly dynamic, and new developments can occur at any time.

I want to stress the importance of making informed decisions when it comes to cryptocurrencies. It's vital to recognize that I am not a registered financial advisor, and this book is not intended to provide specific financial advice. Instead, my goal has been to equip you with the knowledge and tools necessary to make well-informed choices in this rapidly changing field.

Before making any financial decisions related to cryptocurrency, I strongly advise you to do your own research. Double-check the information presented here and stay up to date with the latest developments in the crypto world. Ensure that any investments or decisions you make align with your individual financial goals, risk tolerance, and circumstances.

Additionally, if you come across content or concepts that you find confusing or need further clarification on, please don't hesitate to reach out to me directly. I am always open to helping my readers

and providing additional insights. You can contact me via email at
info.cryptvel@gmail.com

Remember that the cryptocurrency market can be both rewarding and risky. It's a space filled with innovation, but it's also susceptible to rapid changes and fluctuations. Diversification, security practices, and patience are key factors in navigating this world successfully.

Lastly, while financial gains are often a driving force behind cryptocurrency investments, it's essential to be aware of the broader impact and social responsibility that comes with this technology. Consider the potential consequences of your actions on the broader crypto community and society as a whole.

I would like to express my gratitude to you for taking the time to read this book. I hope it has been a valuable resource in your journey through the cryptocurrency landscape. Remember that knowledge is a powerful tool, and your ability to make informed decisions can lead to a more successful and fulfilling experience in the crypto world.

Wishing you all the best in your crypto endeavors, and may your investments be profitable and your decisions well-informed.

Sincerely

Meet Patel

9 798866 704194